Cram101 Textbook Outlines to accompany:

CPC Coding Exam Review 2010 : The Certification Step

Carol J. Buck, 1st Edition

A Content Technologies Inc. publication (c) 2012.

Learning System

Cram101 Textbook Outlines is a learning system. The notes in this book are the highlights of your textbook, you will never have to highlight a book again.

How to use this book. Take this book to class, it is your notebook for the lecture. The notes and highlights on the left hand side of the pages follow the outline and order of the textbook. All you have to do is follow along while your instructor presents the lecture. Circle the items emphasized in class and add other important information on the right side. With Cram101 Textbook Outlines you'll spend less time writing and more time listening. Learning becomes more efficient.

Cram101.com Online

Increase your studying efficiency by using Cram101.com's practice tests and online reference material. It is the perfect complement to Cram101 Textbook Outlines. Use self-teaching matching tests or simulate in-class testing with comprehensive multiple choice tests, or simply use Cram's true and false tests for quick review. Cram101.com even allows you to enter your in-class notes for an integrated studying format combining the textbook notes with your class notes.

Visit **www.Cram101.com**, click Sign Up at the top of the screen, and enter **DK73DW12298** in the promo code box on the registration screen. Your access to www.Cram101.com is discounted by 50% because you have purchased this book. Sign up and stop highlighting textbooks forever.

CPC Coding Exam Review 2010 : The Certification Step
Carol J. Buck, 1st

CONTENTS

Chapter 1. PART I: Chapter 1 - Chapter 4

Dermis	The dermis is a layer of skin between the epidermis and subcutaneous tissues, and is composed of two layers, the papillary and reticular dermis. Structural components of the dermis are collagen, elastic fibers, and extrafibrillar matrix (previously called ground substance).
Epicardium	Epicardium describes the outer layer of heart tissue . When considered as a part of the pericardium, it is the inner layer, or visceral pericardium, continuous with the serous layer. Its largest constituent is connective tissue and functions as a protective layer.
Integumentary system	`Integument` redirects here; in botany, an integument is an outer membrane of an ovule, which later develops into a seed coat. The Integumentary system is the organ system that protects the body from damage, comprising the skin and its appendages . The Integumentary system has a variety of functions; it may serve to waterproof, cushion and protect the deeper tissues, excrete wastes, regulate temperature and is the attachment site for sensory receptors to detect pain, sensation, pressure and temperature.
Nail	A nail is a horn-like structure at the end of a person`s (or an animal`s) finger or toe. The nail is generally regarded as a distinctively primate feature. Although it is not a feature confined exclusively to primates, the development of nails is extremely rare in other mammals.
Sebaceous gland	The Sebaceous glands are microscopic glands in the skin which secrete an oily/waxy matter, called sebum, to lubricate the skin and hair of mammals. In humans, they are found in greatest abundance on the face and scalp, though they are distributed throughout all skin sites except the palms and soles. In the eyelids, meibomian Sebaceous glands secrete sebum into tears.
Subcutaneous tissue	The hypodermis, also called the hypoderm, Subcutaneous tissue, or superficial fascia is the lowermost layer of the integumentary system in vertebrates. Types of cells that are found in the hypodermis are fibroblasts, adipose cells, and macrophages. It is derived from the mesoderm, but unlike the dermis, it is not derived from the dermatome region of the mesoderm.
Sudoriferous glands	Sweat glands also refered to as Sudoriferous glands are exocrine glands, found under the skin of all mammal species, that are used for body temperature regulation. In humans a system of apocrine - and merocrine sweat glands is the main method of cooling. Many other mammals rely on panting or other means as a primary source of cooling, but still use sweat glands to aid in body temperature regulation.

Chapter 1. PART I: Chapter 1 - Chapter 4

Arteries	Arteries are blood vessels that carry blood away from the heart. All Arteries, with the exception of the pulmonary and umbilical Arteries, carry oxygenated blood.
	The circulatory system is extremely important for sustaining life.
Gland	A gland is an organ in an animal`s body that synthesizes a substance for release such as hormones or breast milk, often into the bloodstream (endocrine gland) or into cavities inside the body or its outer surface (exocrine gland).
	glands can be divided into 3 groups:
	· Endocrine glands -- are glands that secrete their products through the basal lamina and lack a duct system.
	· Exocrine glands -- secrete their products through a duct or directly onto the apical surface, the glands in this group can be divided into three groups:
	· Apocrine glands -- a portion of the secreting cell`s body is lost during secretion. Apocrine gland is often used to refer to the apocrine sweat glands, however it is thought that apocrine sweat glands may not be true apocrine glands as they may not use the apocrine method of secretion.
	· Holocrine glands -- the entire cell disintegrates to secrete its substances (e.g., sebaceous glands)
	· Merocrine glands -- cells secrete their substances by exocytosis (e.g., mucous and serous glands). Also called `eccrine.` The type of secretory product of an Exocrine gland may also be one of three categories:
	· Serous glands -- secrete a watery, often protein-rich product.
	· Mucous glands -- secrete a viscous product, rich in carbohydrates (e.g., glycoproteins).

· Sebaceous glands -- secrete a lipid product.
the third type; mixed

Every gland is formed by an ingrowth from an epithelial surface.

Albinism	Albinism is a form of hypopigmentary congenital disorder, characterized by a partial lack or total absence (amelanism or amelanosis) of melanin pigment in the eyes, skin and hair, or more rarely in the eyes alone. Albinism results from inheritance of recessive gene alleles. The condition is known to affect all vertebrates, including humans.
Allograft	Allotransplantation is the transplantation of cells, tissues, or organs, sourced from a genetically non-identical member of the same species as the recipient.. The transplant is called an Allograft or allogeneic transplant or homograft. Most human tissue and organ transplants are Allografts.
Alopecia	Alopecia or hair loss is the medical description of the loss of hair from the head or body, sometimes to the extent of baldness. Unlike the common aesthetic depilation of body hair, Alopecia tends to be involuntary and unwelcome, e.g., androgenic Alopecia. However, it may also be caused by a psychological compulsion to pull out one's own hair (trichotillomania) or the unforeseen consequences of voluntary hairstyling routines .
Anhidrosis	Anhydrosis means lack of sweating. It is also known by a number of other names including Adiaphoresis, Ischidrosis, Hypohidrosis, Oligidria, Oligohidrosis and Sweating deficiency.
	Anhidrosis may be caused by underactivity of the sympathetic nervous system.
Antidiuretic	An Antidiuretic is an agent or drug that, administered to an organism, helps control body water balance by reducing urination, opposing diuresis.
	Antidiuretics are the drugs that reduce urine volume, particularly in diabetes insipidus (DI) which is their primary indication.
	These are classified as:
	· Antidiuretic hormones: ADH/Vasopressin, Desmopressin, Lypressin, Terlipressin

Chapter 1. PART I: Chapter 1 - Chapter 4

	· Miscellaneous: Chlorpropamide, Carbamazepine
Autograft	Autotransplantation is the transplantation of organs, tissues or even proteins from one part of the body to another in the same individual. Tissue transplanted by such 'autologous' procedure is referred to as an Autograft or autotransplant. It is contrasted with xenotransplantation and allotransplantation .
Biopsy	A Biopsy is a medical test involving the removal of cells or tissues for examination. It is the removal of tissue from a living subject to determine the presence or extent of a disease. The tissue is generally examined under a microscope by a pathologist, and can also be analyzed chemically.
Collagen	Collagen is a group of naturally occurring proteins. In nature, it is found exclusively in animals. It is the main protein of connective tissue.
Debridement	Debridement is the medical removal of a patient`s dead, damaged, or infected tissue to improve the healing potential of the remaining healthy tissue. Removal may be surgical, mechanical, chemical, autolytic (self-digestion), and by maggot therapy, where certain species of live maggots selectively eat only necrotic tissue. In oral hygiene and dentistry, Debridement refers to the removal of plaque and calculus that have accumulated on the teeth.
Dermabrasion	Dermabrasion is a cosmetic medical procedure in which the surface of the epidermis of the skin (the stratum corneum) is removed by abrasion (sanding). The instrument used to perform the procedure is called a dermabrader, and that can be any number of types of devices under that category. It is used to remove sun-damaged skin and to remove or lessen scars and dark spots on the skin.
Dermatologist	Dermatology is the branch of medicine dealing with the skin and its diseases, a unique specialty with both medical and surgical aspects. The name of this specialty originated in the form of the (semantically wrong) words dermologie and, a little later, dermatologia . A Dermatologist takes care of diseases, in the widest sense, and some cosmetic problems of the skin, scalp, hair, and nails.
Brachial artery	The Brachial artery is the major blood vessel of the (upper) arm.

	It is the continuation of the axillary artery beyond the lower margin of teres major muscle. It continues down the ventral surface of the arm until it reaches the cubital fossa at the elbow.
Hormone	A Hormone is a chemical released by one or more cells that affects cells in other parts of the organism. Only a small amount of Hormone is required to alter cell metabolism. It is essentially a chemical messenger that transports a signal from one cell to another.
Erythema	Erythema is redness of the skin, which can be caused by several things, including capillary congestion. It can be caused by infection, massage, electrical treatment, acne medication, allergies, exercise, solar radiation (sunburn), cutaneous radiation syndrome, or waxing and plucking of the hairs -- any of which can cause the capillaries to dilate, resulting in redness. Erythema is a common side effect of radiotherapy treatment due to patient exposure to ionizing radiation.
Escharotomy	An Escharotomy is a surgical procedure used to treat full thickness (third-degree) circumferential burns. Since full thickness burns are characterized by tough, leathery eschar, an Escharotomy is used primarily to combat compartment syndrome. Following a full thickness burn, as the underlying tissues are rehydrated, they become constricted due to the eschar`s loss of elasticity, leading to impaired circulation distal to the wound.
Fissure	In anatomy, Fissure is a groove, natural division, deep furrow, cleft, or tear in various parts of the body. Various types of anatomical Fissure are: · Medial longitudinal Fissure or Longitudinal Fissure: which divides the cerebrum into the two hemispheres. · Fissure of Bichat: found below the corpus callosum in the cerebellum of the brain. · Broca`s Fissure: found in the third left frontal fold of the brain.  · Burdach`s Fissure: connects the brain`s insula and the inner surface of the operculum.  · Calcarin`s Fissure: extends from the occipital of the cerebrum to the occipital Fissure. · Callosomarginal Fissure: found in the mesial surface of the cerebrum. · Central Fissure or Rolando`s Fissure: separates the brain`s frontal and parietal lobes.

· Clevenger's Fissure: found in the inferior temporal lobe of the brain

· Collateral Fissure: found in the inferior surface of the cerebrum.

· Hippocampal Fissure: a Fissure that extends from the brain's corpus callosum to the tip of the temporal lobe.

· Horizontal Fissure or Transverse Fissure: found between the cerebrum and the cerebellum. Note that a 'transverse Fissure' can also be found in the liver and lungs.

· Occipitoparietal Fissure: found between the occipital and parietal lobes of the brain.

· Fissure of Sylvius: separates the frontal and parietal lobes of the brain from the temporal lobe.

· Wernicke's Fissure: separates the brain's temporal and parietal lobes from the occipital lobe.

· Zygal Fissure: found in the cerebrum.

· Auricular Fissure: found in the temporal bone

· Pterygomaxillary Fissure

· Sphenoidal Fissure: separates the wings and the body of the sphenoid bone.

· Longitudinal Fissure: found in the lower surface of the liver, also a Fissure that separates the right and left hemispheres of the cerebrum.

· Portal Fissure: found in the under-surface of the liver.

· Umbilical Fissure: found in front of the liver.

· ventral median Fissure

· oblique Fissure of rt ' lf lung

· horizontal Fissure of right lung

· Fissure for ligamentum teres hepatis

	· Fissure for ligamentum venosum
	· Henle`s Fissure: the connective tissue between the muscle fibers of the heart.
	· Palpebral Fissure: separates the upper and lower eyelids. Fissure can also mean unnatural tract or ulcer, most commonly found in the anus.
Hematoma	A Hematoma, or haematoma, is a collection of blood outside the blood vessels, generally the result of hemorrhage, or more specifically, internal bleeding. It is commonly called a bruise.
Ichthyosis	Ichthyosis is a heterogeneous family of at least 28, generalized, mostly genetic skin disorders. All types of Ichthyosis have dry, thickened, scaly or flaky skin. In many types the skin is said to resemble the scales on a fish; the word Ichthyosis comes from the Ancient Greek ιχθΐ ς , meaning `fish.` The severity of symptoms can vary enormously, from the mildest types such as Ichthyosis vulgaris which may be mistaken for normal dry skin up to life-threatening conditions such as harlequin type Ichthyosis.
Leukoderma	Leukoderma is a cutaneous condition, an acquired condition with localized loss of pigmentation of the skin that may occur after any number of inflammatory skin conditions, burns, intralesional steroid injections, postdermabrasion, etc.
Leukoplakia	Leukoplakia is adherent white plaques or patches on the mucous membranes of the oral cavity, including the tongue. The clinical appearance is highly variable. Leukoplakia is not a specific disease entity, but is diagnosis of exclusion.
Lipoma	A Lipoma is a benign tumor composed of fatty tissue. These are the most common form of soft tissue tumor. Lipomas are soft to the touch, usually movable, and are generally painless.
Melanin	Melanin is a class of compounds found in plants, animals, and protists, where it serves predominantly as a pigment. The class of pigments are derivatives of the amino acid tyrosine. Many Melanins are insoluble salts and show affinity to water.
Muscle	Muscle is the contractile tissue of animals and is derived from the mesodermal layer of embryonic germ cells. Muscle cells contain contractile filaments that move past each other and change the size of the cell. They are classified as skeletal, cardiac, or smooth Muscles.

Chapter 1. PART I: Chapter 1 - Chapter 4

Sebum	The sebaceous glands are microscopic glands in the skin which secrete an oily/waxy matter, called Sebum, to lubricate the skin and hair of animals. In humans, they are found in greatest abundance on the face and scalp, though they are distributed throughout all skin sites except the palms and soles. In the eyelids, meibomian sebaceous glands secrete Sebum into tears.
Xanthoma	A Xanthoma is a deposition of yellowish cholesterol-rich material in tendons and other body parts in various disease states. Tendon Xanthoma are associated with Type II hyperlipidaemia Palmar Xanthomata and tuboeruptive Xanthomata occur in Type III hyperlipidaemia
Disease	A Disease or medical condition is an abnormal condition of an organism that impairs bodily functions, associated with specific symptoms and signs. It may be caused by external factors, such as invading organisms, or it may be caused by internal dysfunctions, such as autoimmune Diseases. In human beings, `Disease` is often used more broadly to refer to any condition that causes pain, dysfunction, distress, social problems, and/or death to the person afflicted, or similar problems for those in contact with the person.
Frenulum	A Frenulum is a small fold of tissue that secures or restricts the motion of a mobile organ in the body. Frenula on the human body include several in the mouth, some in the digestive tract, and some connected to the external genitalia. · Oral tissue: Frenula of the mouth include the Frenulum linguae under the tongue, the Frenulum labii superioris inside the upper lip, the Frenulum labii inferioris inside the lower lip, and the buccal frena which connect the cheeks to the gum. These can easily be torn by violent blows to the face or mouth, thus a torn Frenulum is sometimes a warning sign of physical abuse. · Vulvular tissue: In females, genital frenula include the Frenulum clitoridis of the clitoris and the Frenulum labiorum pudendi (aka fourchette) where the labia minora meet at the back.

· Penile tissue: The word Frenulum on its own is often used for the Frenulum of prepuce of penis or Frenulum preputii penis, which is an elastic band of tissue under the glans penis that connects to the prepuce, or foreskin to the vernal mucosa, and helps contract the prepuce over the glans.

· Brain: Frenulum veli
An overly short oral or genital Frenulum may require a frenectomy or frenuloplasty to achieve normal mobility.

Surgery	Surgery is a medical specialty that uses operative manual and instrumental techniques on a patient to investigate and/or treat a pathological condition such as disease or injury, to help improve bodily function or appearance, and sometimes for religious reasons. An act of performing Surgery may be called a surgical procedure, operation, or simply Surgery. In this context, the verb operating means performing Surgery.
Macule	A Macule is a change in epidermis color, without elevation or depression and, therefore, nonpalpable, well or ill-defined, variously sized but, by convention, less than ten milimeters in diameter at the widest point. This skin lesion is recognizable due to the color difference compared with the surrounding normal skin, and may be of any color, white, blue, or red for example. Macules may be the result of hyperpigmentation, hypopigmentation, vascular abnormalities, capillary dilatation (erythema), or purpura (extravasated red blood cells).
Papule	A Papule is a circumscribed, solid elevation of skin with no visible fluid, varying in size from a pinhead to 1 cm. They can be either brown, purple, pink or red in colour. The Papules may open when scratched and become infected and crusty.
Purkinje fibers	Purkinje fibers are a unique end organ cardiac extension of the Autonomic Nervous System. Given further histologic examination, these fibers are split into left and right trees as well as atrial and ventricular contributions. The electrical origin of atrial Purkinje fibers arrives from the Sinoatrial Node.
Tumor	A tumor or tumour is the name for a swelling or lesion formed by an abnormal growth of cells (termed neoplastic). tumor is not synonymous with cancer. A tumor can be benign, pre-malignant or malignant, whereas cancer is by definition malignant.

Chapter 1. PART I: Chapter 1 - Chapter 4

Pathophysiology	Pathophysiology is the study of the changes of normal mechanical, physical, and biochemical functions, either caused by a disease, or resulting from an abnormal syndrome. More formally, it is the branch of medicine which deals with any disturbances of body functions, caused by disease or prodromal symptoms. An alternate definition is `the study of the biological and physical manifestations of disease as they correlate with the underlying abnormalities and physiological disturbances.` The study of pathology and the study of Pathophysiology often involves substantial overlap in diseases and processes, but pathology emphasizes direct observations, while Pathophysiology emphasizes quantifiable measurements.
Atrophy	Atrophy is the partial or complete wasting away of a part of the body. Causes of Atrophy include poor nourishment, poor circulation, loss of hormonal support, loss of nerve supply to the target organ, disuse or lack of exercise or disease intrinsic to the tissue itself. Hormonal and nerve inputs that maintain an organ or body part are referred to as trophic [noun] in medical practice.
Pressure	Example reading: $1 \text{ Pa} = 1 \text{ N/m}^2 = 10^{-5}$ bar $= 10.197 \times 10^{-6}$ at $= 9.8692 \times 10^{-6}$ atm, etc. As an example of varying Pressures, a finger can be pressed against a wall without making any lasting impression; however, the same finger pushing a thumbtack can easily damage the wall. Although the force applied to the surface is the same, the thumbtack applies more Pressure because the point concentrates that force into a smaller area.
Bedsores	Bedsores, more properly known as pressure ulcers or decubitus ulcers, are lesions caused by many factors such as: unrelieved pressure; friction; humidity; shearing forces; temperature; age; continence and medication; to any part of the body, especially portions over bony or cartilaginous areas such as sacrum, elbows, knees, ankles etc. Although easily prevented and completely treatable if found early, Bedsores are often fatal - even under the auspices of medical care - and are one of the leading iatrogenic causes of death reported in developed countries, second only to adverse drug reactions. Prior to the 1950s, treatment was ineffective until Doreen Norton showed that the primary cure and treatment was to remove the pressure by turning the patient every two hours.

Chapter 1. PART I: Chapter 1 - Chapter 4

Keloid	A Keloid (also known as a `Keloidal scar`:[1499]) is a type of scar, which depending on its maturity, is composed of mainly either type III (early) or type I(late) collagen. It is a result of an overgrowth of granulation tissue (collagen type 3) at the site of a healed skin injury which is then slowly replaced by collagen type 1. Keloids are firm, rubbery lesions or shiny, fibrous nodules, and can vary from pink to flesh-colored or red to dark brown in color.
Atopic dermatitis	Atopic dermatitis is an inflammatory, chronically relapsing, non-contagious and pruritic skin disease. It has been given names like 'prurigo Besnier,' 'neurodermitis,' 'endogenous eczema,' 'flexural eczema,' 'infantile eczema,' and 'prurigo diathsique'. The skin of a patient with Atopic dermatitis reacts abnormally and easily to irritants, food, and environmental allergens and becomes red, flaky and very itchy.
Contact dermatitis	Contact dermatitis or Irritant dermatitis is a term for a skin reaction resulting from exposure to allergens (allergic Contact dermatitis) or irritants (irritant Contact dermatitis). Phototoxic dermatitis occurs when the allergen or irritant is activated by sunlight. Contact dermatitis is a localized rash or irritation of the skin caused by contact with a foreign substance.
Dermatitis	Dermatitis is a blanket term meaning `inflammation of the skin` (e.g. rash). There are several different types of Dermatitis. The different kinds usually have in common an allergic reaction to specific allergens.
Leukemia	Leukemia is a cancer of the blood or bone marrow and is characterized by an abnormal proliferation (production by multiplication) of blood cells, usually white blood cells (leukocytes). Leukemia is a broad term covering a spectrum of diseases. In turn, it is part of the even broader group of diseases called hematological neoplasms.
Irritant contact dermatitis	Irritant contact dermatitis is a form of contact dermatitis that can be divided into forms caused by chemical irritants and those caused by physical irritants. Chemical Irritant contact dermatitis is either acute or chronic, which is usually associated with strong and weak irritants respectively (HSE MS24). The following definition is provided by Mathias and Maibach (1978): a nonimmunologic local inflammatory reaction characterized by erythema, edema, or corrosion following single or repeated application of a chemical substance to an identical cutaneous site.

Chapter 1. PART I: Chapter 1 - Chapter 4

Psoriasis	Psoriasis is a chronic, non-contagious disease that affects mainly the skin. It is currently suspected to be autoimmune in origin. It commonly causes red, scaly patches to appear on the skin, although some patients have no dermatological symptoms.
Lichen planus	Lichen planus is a chronic mucocutaneous disease that affects the skin and the oral mucosa, and presents itself in the form of papules, lesions or rashes. Lichen planus doesn't involve lichens; the name refers to the appearance of affected skin.
	Lichen planus may be divided into the following types:[466]
	· Configuration
	· Annular Lichen planus
	· Linear Lichen planus
	· Morphology of lesion
	· Hypertrophic Lichen planus
	· Atrophic Lichen planus
	· Vesiculobullous Lichen planus
	· Ulcerative Lichen planus
	· Follicular Lichen planus

· Actinic Lichen planus

· Lichen planus pigmentosus

· Site of involvement

· Lichen planus of the palms and soles (Palmoplantar Lichen planus)

· Mucosal Lichen planus

· Lichen planus of the nails

· Lichen planus of the scalp

· Inverse Lichen planus

· Special forms

· Drug-induced Lichen planus

· Lupus erythematosus-Lichen planus overlap syndrome

· Lichen planus pemphigoides

· Keratosis lichenoides chronica

· Lichenoid reaction of graft-versus-host disease

	· Lichenoid keratosis
	· Lichenoid dermatitis
	The cause of Lichen planus is not known. It is not contagious and does not involve any known pathogen.
Luteinizing hormone	Luteinizing hormone is a hormone produced by the anterior pituitary gland.
	· In the female, an acute rise of Luteinizing hormone - the Luteinizing hormone surge - triggers ovulation and corpus luteum development.
	· In the male, where Luteinizing hormone had also been called Interstitial Cell Stimulating Hormone , it stimulates Leydig cell production of testosterone. Luteinizing hormone is a heterodimeric glycoprotein. Each monomeric unit is a glycoprotein molecule; one alpha and one beta subunit make the full, functional protein.
Pityriasis rosea	Pityriasis rosea is an acute, self-limiting skin eruption with a distinctive and constant course, with an initial lesion or grouping of lesions ('herald patch') that is a primary plaque that is followed after 1 or 2 weeks by a generalized, much more spread, secondary rash with a typical distribution and lasting for about 6 weeks. [445:208-9] A medical source describes the condition as non-contagious, however another source says only that it is 'non-contagious in the classic sense' and a third does not speak to the question.
	Pityriasis rosea can affect members of either sex, at any age.
	The symptoms of this condition include:
	Herald lesion of Pityriasis rosea (second lesion above the ankle, approximately in the center of the plate) depicted 21 days after initial encounter.

Chapter 1. PART I: Chapter 1 - Chapter 4

Acne vulgaris	Acne vulgaris is a common human skin disease, characterized by areas of skin with multiple noninflammatory follicular papules or comedones and by inflammatory papules, pustules, and nodules in its more severe forms. Acne vulgaris mostly affects the areas of skin with the densest population of sebaceous follicles; these areas include the face, the upper part of the chest, and the back. Severe acne is inflammatory, but acne can also manifest in noninflammatory forms.
Impetigo	Impetigo is a superficial bacterial skin infection most common among school children. People who play close contact sports such as rugby, American football and wrestling are also susceptible, regardless of age. Impetigo is not as common in adults.
Cervical	In anatomy, `Cervical` is an adjective that has two meanings: · of or pertaining to any neck. · of or pertaining to the female cervix: i.e., the neck of the uterus. · Commonly used medical phrases involving the neck are · Cervical collar · Cervical disc (intervertebral disc) · Cervical lymph nodes · Cervical nerves · Cervical vertebrae · Cervical rib · Phrases that involve the cervix include

	· Cervical cancer
	· Cervical smear or Pap smear
Disease	A Disease or medical condition is an abnormal condition of an organism that impairs bodily functions, associated with specific symptoms and signs. It may be caused by external factors, such as invading organisms, or it may be caused by internal dysfunctions, such as autoimmune Diseases. In human beings, `Disease` is often used more broadly to refer to any condition that causes pain, dysfunction, distress, social problems, and/or death to the person afflicted, or similar problems for those in contact with the person.
Infection	An Infection is the detrimental colonization of a host organism by a foreign species. In an Infection, the infecting organism seeks to utilize the host`s resources to multiply, usually at the expense of the host. The infecting organism, or pathogen, interferes with the normal functioning of the host and can lead to chronic wounds, gangrene, loss of an infected limb, and even death.
Vertebra	A Vertebra are is an individual bone in the flexible column that defines Vertebrate animals, e.g. humans. The Vertebral column encases and protects the spinal cord, which runs from the base of the cranium down the dorsal side of the animal until reaching the pelvis. From there, Vertebra continue into the tail.
Boil	Boil is a skin disease caused by the infection of hair follicles, resulting in the localized accumulation of pus and dead tissue. Individual Boils can cluster together and form an interconnected network of Boils called carbuncles. Boils are red, pus-filled lumps that are tender, warm, and extremely painful.
Cellulitis	Cellulitis is a diffuse inflammation of connective tissue with severe inflammation of dermal and subcutaneous layers of the skin. Cellulitis can be caused by normal skin flora or by exogenous bacteria, and often occurs where the skin has previously been broken: cracks in the skin, cuts, blisters, burns, insect bites, surgical wounds, or sites of intravenous catheter insertion. Skin on the face or lower legs is most commonly affected by this infection, though Cellulitis can occur on any part of the body.
Erysipelas	Erysipelas is an acute streptococcus bacterial infection of the dermis, resulting in inflammation.

	This disease is most common among the elderly, infants, and children. People with immune deficiency, diabetes, alcoholism, skin ulceration, fungal infections and impaired lymphatic drainage (e.g., after mastectomy, pelvic surgery, bypass grafting) are also at increased risk.
Folliculitis	Folliculitis is the inflammation of one or more hair follicles. The condition may occur anywhere on the skin. Most carbuncles, furuncles, and other cases of Folliculitis develop from Staphylococcus aureus.
Herpes simplex	Herpes simplex is a viral disease caused by both Herpes simplex virus 1 (HSV-1) and Herpes simplex virus 2 (HSV-2). Infection with the herpes virus is categorized into one of several distinct disorders based on the site of infection. Oral herpes, the visible symptoms of which are colloquially called cold sores, infects the face and mouth.
Herpes simplex virus	Herpes simplex virus 1 and 2 (Herpes simplex virus-1 and Herpes simplex virus-2), also known as Human herpes virus 1 and 2 (HHV-1 and -2), are two members of the herpes virus family, Herpesviridae, that infect humans. Both Herpes simplex virus-1 and -2 are ubiquitous and contagious. They can be spread when an infected person is producing and shedding the virus.
Fasciitis	In medicine, Fasciitis refers to an inflammation of the fascia. In particular, it often refers to one of the following diseases: · Necrotizing Fasciitis · Plantar Fasciitis · Eosinophilic Fasciitis

---

· Paraneoplastic Fasciitis

Noncapsular joint
Nonjoint
Chronic
Processes
Specific types

Necrotizing fasciitis	Necrotizing fasciitis, commonly known as flesh-eating disease or flesh-eating bacteria, is a rare infection of the deeper layers of skin and subcutaneous tissues, easily spreading across the fascial plane within the subcutaneous tissue. Type I describes a polymicrobial infection, whereas Type II describes a monomicrobial infection. Many types of bacteria can cause Necrotizing fasciitis (e.g., Group A streptococcus (Streptococcus pyogenes), Staphylococcus aureus, Vibrio vulnificus, Clostridium perfringens, Bacteroides fragilis).
Herpes zoster	Herpes zoster, commonly known as shingles and also known as zona, is a viral disease characterized by a painful skin rash with blisters in a limited area on one side of the body, often in a stripe. The initial infection with varicella zoster virus (VZV) causes the acute (short-lived) illness chickenpox, and generally occurs in children and young people. Once an episode of chickenpox has resolved, the virus is not eliminated from the body but can go on to cause shingles--an illness with very different symptoms--often many years after the initial infection.
Wart	A Wart is generally a small, rough tumor, typically on hands and feet but often other locations, that can resemble a cauliflower or a solid blister. Warts are common, and are caused by a viral infection, specifically by the human papillomavirus (HPV) and are contagious when in contact with the skin of an infected person. It is also possible to get Warts from using towels or other objects used by an infected person.

Chapter 1. PART I: Chapter 1 - Chapter 4

Candidiasis	Candidiasis or thrush is a fungal infection (mycosis) of any of the Candida species, of which Candida albicans is the most common. Candidiasis encompasses infections that range from superficial, such as oral thrush and vaginitis, to systemic and potentially life-threatening diseases. Candida infections of the latter category are also referred to as candidemia and are usually confined to severely immunocompromised persons, such as cancer, transplant, and AIDS patients.
Plantar wart	A Plantar wart (also known as `Verruca plantaris`[405]) is a wart caused by the human papillomavirus (HPV) occurring on the sole or toes of the foot. . Plantar warts are usually self-limiting, but should be treated to lessen symptoms (which may include pain), decrease duration, and reduce transmission.
Right	Rights are variously construed as legal, social, or moral freedoms to act or refrain from acting, or entitlements to be acted upon or not acted upon. While the concept is fundamental to civilized societies, there is considerable disagreement about what is meant precisely by the term Rights. It has been used by different groups and thinkers for different purposes, with different and sometimes opposing definitions, and the precise definition of the concept, beyond having something to do with normative rules of some sort or another, is controversial.
Right atrium	The Right atrium is one of four chambers (two atria and two ventricles) in the hearts of mammals (including humans) and archosaurs (which include birds and crocodilians). It receives deoxygenated blood from the superior and inferior vena cava and the coronary sinus, and pumps it into the right ventricle through the tricuspid valve. Attached to the Right atrium is the right auricular appendix.
Right ventricle	The Right ventricle is one of four chambers (two atria and two ventricles) in the human heart. It receives deoxygenated blood from the right atrium via the tricuspid valve, and pumps it into the pulmonary artery via the pulmonary valve and pulmonary trunk. It is triangular in form, and extends from the right atrium to near the apex of the heart.
Tinea	Seek medical attention asap Tinea is a general term used to describe skin mycoses. The term ringworm is even less precise, but is usually considered a synonym.

	It is sometimes equated with dermatophytosis, and it is true that most conditions identified as `Tinea` are members of the imperfect fungi that make up the dermatophytes.
Tinea capitis	Tinea capitis is a superficial fungal infection (dermatophytosis) of the scalp. The disease is primarily caused by dermatophytes in the Trichophyton and Microsporum genera that invade the hair shaft. The clinical presentation is typically a single or multiple patches of hair loss, sometimes with a `black dot` pattern (often with broken-off hairs), that may be accompanied by inflammation, scaling, pustules, and itching.
Tinea corporis	Tinea corporis is a superficial fungal infection (dermatophytosis) of the arms and legs, especially on glabrous skin, however it may occur on any part of the body.
Actinic keratosis	Actinic keratosis is a premalignant condition of thick, scaly, or crusty patches of skin.[719] It is more common in fair-skinned people. It is associated with those who are frequently exposed to the sun, as it is usually accompanied by solar damage. Since some of these pre-cancers progress to squamous cell carcinoma, they should be treated.
Adrenocorticotropic hormone	Adrenocorticotropic hormone is a polypeptide tropic hormone produced and secreted by the anterior pituitary gland. It is an important component of the hypothalamic-pituitary-adrenal axis and is often produced in response to biological stress . Its principal effects are increased production of corticosteroids and, as its name suggests, cortisol from the adrenal cortex.
Seborrheic keratosis	A Seborrheic keratosis is a noncancerous benign skin growth that originates in keratinocytes. Like liver spots, seborrheic keratoses are seen more often as people age. In fact they are sometimes humorously referred to as the `barnacles of old age`.
Squamous cell carcinoma	In medicine, squamous cell carcinoma is a form of cancer of the carcinoma type that may occur in many different organs, including the skin, lips, mouth, esophagus, urinary bladder, prostate, lungs, vagina, and cervix. It is a malignant tumor of squamous epithelium (epithelium that shows squamous cell differentiation). squamous cell carcinoma may be classified into the following types:[473] · Adenoid squamous cell carcinoma · Clear cell squamous cell carcinoma

· Spindle cell squamous cell carcinoma

· Signet-ring cell squamous cell carcinoma

· Basaloid squamous cell carcinoma

· Verrucous carcinoma

· Keratoacanthoma

A carcinoma can be characterized as either in situ (confined to the original site) or invasive, depending on whether the cancer invades underlying tissues; only invasive cancers are able to spread to other organs and cause metastasis. squamous cell carcinoma in situ are also called Bowen's disease.

· Erythroplasia of Queyrat

· Keratoacanthoma is a low-grade malignancy of the skin.

Carcinoma	A Carcinoma is any malignant cancer that arises from epithelial cells. Carcinomas invade surrounding tissues and organs and may metastasize, or spread, to lymph nodes and other sites. Carcinoma in situ (CIS) is a pre-malignant condition, in which some cytological signs of malignancy are present, but there is no histological evidence of invasion through the epithelial basement membrane.
Syndrome	In medicine and psychology, the term syndrome refers to the association of several clinically recognizable features, signs (observed by a physician), symptoms (reported by the patient), phenomena or characteristics that often occur together, so that the presence of one feature alerts the physician to the presence of the others. In recent decades the term has been used outside of medicine to refer to a combination of phenomena seen in association. The term syndrome derives from its Greek roots and means literally `run together`, as the features do.

Chapter 1. PART I: Chapter 1 - Chapter 4

Basal cell carcinoma	Basal cell carcinoma is the most common type of skin cancer. It rarely metastasizes or kills, but it is still considered malignant because it can cause significant destruction and disfigurement by invading surrounding tissues. Statistically, approximately 3 out of 10 Caucasians develop a basal cell cancer within their lifetime.
Melanoma	Melanoma is a malignant tumor of melanocytes which are found predominantly in skin but also in the bowel and the eye . It is one of the less common types of skin cancer but causes the majority (75%) of skin cancer related deaths. Melanocytes are normally present in skin, being responsible for the production of the dark pigment melanin.
Sarcoma	A Sarcoma is a cancer of the connective tissue resulting in mesoderm proliferation. This is in contrast to carcinomas, which are of epithelial origin (breast, colon, pancreas, and others). However, due to an evolving understanding of tissue origin, the term `Sarcoma` is sometimes applied to tumors now known to arise from epithelial tissue.
Long bones	The Long bones are those that are longer than they are wide, and grow primarily by elongation of the diaphysis, with an epiphysis at the ends of the growing bone. The ends of epiphyses are covered with a hyaline cartilage (`articular cartilage`). The longitudinal growth of Long bones is a result of endochondral ossification at the epiphyseal plate.
Musculoskeletal system	A Musculoskeletal system is an organ system that gives animals (including humans) the ability to move using the muscular and skeletal systems. The Musculoskeletal system provides form, stability, and movement to the body. It is made up of the body`s bones (the skeleton), muscles, cartilage, tendons, ligaments, joints, and other connective tissue (the tissue that supports and binds tissues and organs together).
Bone	Bones are rigid organs that form part of the endoskeleton of vertebrates. They function to move, support, and protect the various organs of the body, produce red and white blood cells and store minerals. bone tissue is a type of dense connective tissue.
Axial	Axial has different meanings: · In geometry, it means: along the same line as an axis (coAxial) or centerline: parallel (geometry), contrary to radial, perpendicular or tangential · In anatomy, it relates to an anatomical direction of animals and humans

Chapter 1. PART I: Chapter 1 - Chapter 4

	· In the skeletal system, the Axial skeleton refers to the system of bones oriented vertically along the longitudinal axis
	· In music, it is a type of modal frame
	· In chemistry, it relates to an Axial bond or the vertical axis of a flat molecule, the opposite of equatorial
	· Historically, the Axial age refers to the period from 800 to 200 BC during which intense intellectual development occurred in three different regions: China, India and the Occident
Axial skeleton	The Axial skeleton consists of the 80 bones in the head and trunk of the human body. It is composed of five parts; the human skull, the ossicles of the inner ear, the hyoid bone of the throat, the rib cage, and the vertebral column. The Axial skeleton and the appendicular skeleton together form the complete skeleton.
Appendicular skeleton	The Appendicular skeleton is composed of 126 bones in the human body. The word appendicular is the adjective of the noun appendage which itself means a part that is joined to something larger. Functionally it is involved in locomotion (Lower limbs) of the axial skeleton and manipulation of objects in the environment (Upper limbs).
Muscular system	Myology is the specialised study of muscles and muscle tissue.
	The muscular system consists of skeletal muscles that act (contract) to move or position parts of the body (e.g., the bones that articulate at joints), or smooth and cardiac muscle that propels, expels, or controls the flow of fluids and contained substance.
Brachioradialis	Brachioradialis is a muscle of the forearm that acts to flex the forearm at the elbow. It is also capable of both pronation and supination, depending on the position of the forearm; for this reason it is also called 'the beer drinker muscle.' It is attached to the distal styloid process of the radius by way of the Brachioradialis tendon, and to the lateral supracondylar ridge of the humerus.
	Brachioradialis flexes the forearm at the elbow.

Chapter 1. PART I: Chapter 1 - Chapter 4

Occipital bone	The Occipital bone, a saucer-shaped membrane bone situated at the back and lower part of the cranium, is trapezoid in shape and curved on itself. It is pierced by a large oval aperture, the foramen magnum, through which the cranial cavity communicates with the vertebral canal. · The curved, expanded plate behind the foramen magnum is named the squama occipitalis. · The thick, somewhat quadrilateral piece in front of the foramen is called the basilar part of Occipital bone. · On either side of the foramen are the lateral parts of Occipital bone. .
Pronation	In anatomy, Pronation is a rotational movement of the forearm at the radioulnar joint, or of the foot at the subtalar and talocalcaneonavicular joints. For the forearm, when standing in the anatomical position, Pronation will move the palm of the hand from an anterior-facing position to a posterior-facing position without an associated movement at the shoulder (glenohumeral joint). This corresponds to a counterclockwise twist for the right forearm and a clockwise twist for the left.
Supination	Supination is a position of either the forearm or foot; in the forearm when the palm faces anteriorly, or faces up (when the arms are unbent and at the sides). Supination in the foot occurs when a person appears `bow-legged` with their weight supported primarily on the anterior of their feet The hand is supine (facing anteriorly) in the anatomical position. This action is performed by the Biceps brachii and the Supinator muscle.
Temporal bone	The Temporal bones are situated at the sides and base of the skull, and lateral to the temporal lobes of the cerebrum. The Temporal bone supports that part of the face known as the temple.

The Temporal bone consists of four parts:

· Squama temporalis

· Mastoid portion

· Petrous portion (Petrosal ridge)

· Tympanic part
The structure of the squama is like that of the other cranial bones: the mastoid portion is spongy, and the petrous portion dense and hard.

In evolutionary terms, the Temporal bone is derived from the fusion of many bones that are often separate in non-human mammals:

· The squamosal bone, which is homologous with the squama, and forms the side of the cranium in many bony fish and tetrapods. Primitively, it is a flattened plate-like bone, but in many animals it is narrower in form, for example, where it forms the boundary between the two temporal fenestrae of diapsid reptiles.

· The petrous and mastoid parts of the Temporal bone, which derive from the periotic bone, formed from the fusion of a number of bones surrounding the ear of reptiles.

Joint	A Joint is the location at which two or more bones make contact. They are constructed to allow movement and provide mechanical support, and are classified structurally and functionally. Joints are mainly classified structurally and functionally.
Placenta	The Placenta is an organ that connects the developing fetus to the uterine wall to allow nutrient uptake, waste elimination and gas exchange via the mother`s blood supply. Placentas are a defining characteristic of eutherian or `Placental` mammals, but are also found in some snakes and lizards with varying levels of development up to mammalian levels. The word Placenta comes from the Latin for cake, from Greek plakóenta/plakoúnta, accusative of plakóeis/plakoús - πλακΪŒεις, πλακοΪ ς, `flat, slab-like`, in reference to its round, flat appearance in humans.

Chapter 1. PART I: Chapter 1 - Chapter 4

Achilles tendon	The Achilles tendon, also known as the calcaneal tendon or the tendo calcaneus, is a tendon of the posterior leg. It serves to attach the plantaris, gastrocnemius and soleus muscles to the calcaneus (heel) bone. The Achilles is the tendonous extension of three muscles in the lower leg: gastrocnemius, soleus, and plantaris.
Pectoralis major	The pectoralis major is a thick, fan-shaped muscle, situated at the chest of the body. It makes up the bulk of the chest muscles in the male and lies under the breast in the female. Underneath the pectoralis major is the pectoralis minor, a thin, triangular muscle.
Transverse	The transverse or costal processes of a vertebra, two in number, project one at either side from the point where the lamina joins the pedicle, between the superior and inferior articular processes. They serve for the attachment of muscles and ligaments.
Auditory	Auditory means of or relating to the process of hearing: · Auditory system, the neurological structures and pathways of sound perception. · Sound, the physical signal perceived by the Auditory system. · Hearing (sense), is the Auditory sense, the sense by which sound is perceived. · Ear, the Auditory end organ. · Cochlea, the Auditory branch of the inner ear. · Auditory illusion, sound trick analogous to an optical illusion. · Primary Auditory cortex, the part of the higher-level of the brain that serves hearing. · External Auditory meatus, the ear canal · Auditory scene analysis, the process by which a scene containing many sounds is perceived · Auditory phonetics, the science of the sounds of language

	· Auditory imagery, hearing in head in the absence of sound
Canal	Canals are man-made channels for water. There are two types of Canal:
	· Aqueduct Canals that are used for the conveyance and delivery of fresh water, for human consumption, agriculture, etc. · Waterway Canals that are navigable transportation Canals used for carrying ships and boats loaded with goods and people, often connected to existing lakes, rivers, or oceans. Included here are inter-ocean Canals such as the Suez Canal and the Panama Canal. The word `Canal` is also used for a city-Canal in Dutch cities.
Carotid arteries	In human anatomy, the common carotid artery is an artery that supplies the head and neck with oxygenated blood; it divides in the neck to form the external and internal Carotid arteries. The common carotid artery is a paired structure, meaning that there are two in the body, one for each half. The left and right common Carotid arteries follow the same course with the exception of their origin.
Colon	The colon is the last part of the digestive system in most vertebrates; it extracts water and salt from solid wastes before they are eliminated from the body, and is the site in which flora-aided (largely bacteria) fermentation of unabsorbed material occurs. Unlike the small intestine, the colon does not play a major role in absorption of foods and nutrients. However, the colon does absorb water, potassium and some fat soluble vitamins.
Ductus arteriosus	In the developing fetus, the Ductus arteriosus also called the ductus Botalli or ductus Layton in the United Kingdom, is a shunt connecting the pulmonary artery to the aortic arch. It allows most of the blood from the right ventricle to bypass the fetus` fluid-filled lungs, protecting the lungs from being overworked and allowing the left ventricle to strengthen. There are two other fetal shunts, the ductus venosus and the foramen ovale.
Major	Major is a rank of commissioned officer, with corresponding ranks existing in almost every military in the world.

	When used unhyphenated, in conjunction with no other indicator of rank, the term refers to the rank just senior to that of an Army captain and just below the rank of lieutenant colonel. It is considered the most junior of the field ranks.
Patent	A Patent is a set of exclusive rights granted by a state (national government) to an inventor or their assignee for a limited period of time in exchange for a public disclosure of an invention.
	The procedure for granting Patents, the requirements placed on the Patentee, and the extent of the exclusive rights vary widely between countries according to national laws and international agreements. Typically, however, a Patent application must include one or more claims defining the invention which must be new, non-obvious, and useful or industrially applicable.
Tendons	A tendon is a tough band of fibrous connective tissue that usually connects muscle to bone and is capable of withstanding tension. Tendons are similar to ligaments and fascia as they are all made of collagen except that ligaments join one bone to another bone, and fascia connect muscles to other muscles. Tendons and muscles work together and can only exert a pulling force.
Arthrocentesis	Arthrocentesis is the clinical procedure of using a syringe to collect synovial fluid from a joint capsule. It is also known as joint aspiration. Arthrocentesis is used in the diagnosis of gout, arthritis, and synovial infections.
Arthrodesis	Arthrodesis is the artificial induction of joint ossification between two bones via surgery. This is done to relieve intractable pain in a joint which cannot be managed by pain medication, splints, or other normally-indicated treatments. The typical causes of such pain are fractures which disrupt the joint, and arthritis.
Arthroplasty	Joint replacement consists of replacing painful, arthritic, worn or cancerous parts of the joint with artificial surfaces shaped in such a way as to allow joint movement.
	Arthroplasty [from Greek arthron, joint, limb, articulate, + -plassein, to form, mould, forge, feign, make an image of] is a procedure of orthopedic surgery, in which the arthritic or dysfunctional joint surface is replaced with something better or by remodelling or realigning the joint by osteotomy or some other procedure.

	Previously, a popular form of Arthroplasty was interpositional Arthroplasty with interposition of some other tissue like skin, muscle or tendon to keep inflammatory surfaces apart or excisional Arthroplasty in which the joint surface and bone was removed leaving scar tissue to fill in the gap.
Arthroscopy	Arthroscopy is a minimally invasive surgical procedure in which an examination and sometimes treatment of damage of the interior of a joint is performed using an arthroscope, a type of endoscope that is inserted into the joint through a small incision. Arthroscopic procedures can be performed either to evaluate or to treat many orthopaedic conditions including torn floating cartilage, torn surface cartilage, ACL reconstruction, and trimming damaged cartilage. The advantage of Arthroscopy over traditional open surgery is that the joint does not have to be opened up fully.
Articular	The Articular bone is part of the lower jaw of most tetrapods, including amphibians, sauropsids ('reptiles'), birds and early synapsids. In these animals it is connected to two other lower jaw bones, the suprangular and the angular. It forms the jaw joint by articulating with the quadrate bone of the skull.
Bunion	A Bunion is a structural deformity of the bones and the joint between the foot and big toe, and may be painful. A Bunion is an enlargement of bone or tissue around the joint at the base of the big toe (metatarsophalangeal joint).The big toe may turn in toward the second toe (angulation), and the tissues surrounding the joint may be swollen and tender. Today the term usually is used to refer to the pathological bump on the side of the great toe joint.
Bursitis	Bursitis is the inflammation of one or more bursae (small sacs) of synovial fluid in the body. The bursae rest at the points where internal functionaries, such as muscles and tendons, slide across bone. Healthy bursae create a smooth, almost frictionless functional gliding surface making normal movement painless.
Carpal tunnel syndrome	Carpal tunnel syndrome is a medical condition in which the median nerve is compressed at the wrist, leading to paresthesias, numbness and muscle weakness in the hand. Night symptoms and waking at night are characteristic of established Carpal tunnel syndrome. They can be managed effectively with night-time wrist splinting in most patients.

Chapter 1. PART I: Chapter 1 - Chapter 4

Dislocations	In materials science, a dislocation is a crystallographic defect, or irregularity, within a crystal structure. The presence of Dislocations strongly influences many of the properties of materials. The theory was originally developed by Vito Volterra in 1905. Some types of Dislocations can be visualized as being caused by the termination of a plane of atoms in the middle of a crystal.
Fracture	A fracture is the (local) separation of an object or material into two, or more, pieces under the action of stress. The word fracture is often applied to bones of living creatures, or to crystals or crystalline materials, such as gemstones or metal. Sometimes, in crystalline materials, individual crystals fracture without the body actually separating into two or more pieces.
Foramen	In anatomy, a Foramen is any opening. Many foramina transmit muscle or a nerve.
Fovea	The term Fovea comes from the Latin, meaning pit or pitfall. As an anatomical term, there are several Foveae around the body, including in the head of the femur. The Fovea centralis, also generally known as the Fovea, is a part of the eye, located in the center of the macula region of the retina.
Fovea centralis	The term fovea comes from the Latin, meaning pit or pitfall. As an anatomical term, there are several foveae around the body, including in the head of the femur. The fovea centralis, also generally known as the fovea, is a part of the eye, located in the center of the macula region of the retina.
Ganglion	In anatomy, a Ganglion is a biological tissue mass, most commonly a mass of nerve cell bodies. Cells found in a Ganglion are called Ganglion cells, though this term is also sometimes used to refer specifically to retinal Ganglion cells. In some dinosaurs, the Ganglion in the pelvis was so large relative to its brain that it could almost be said to have two brains.

Kyphosis	Kyphosis , also called hunchback, is a common condition of a curvature of the upper spine. It can be either the result of degenerative diseases , developmental problems, osteoporosis with compression fractures of the vertebrae, and/or trauma.
	In the sense of a deformity, it is the pathological curving of the spine, where parts of the spinal column lose some or all of their lordotic profile.
Lactiferous duct	Lactiferous ducts lead from the lobules of the mammary gland to the tip of the nipple. They are also referred to as galactophores, galactophorous ducts, mammary ducts, mamillary ducts and milk ducts. They are structures which carry milk toward the nipple in a lactating female.
Ligament	In anatomy, the term Ligament is used to denote three different types of structures:
	· Fibrous tissue that connects bones to other bones. They are sometimes called `articular Ligaments`, `fibrous Ligaments`, or `true Ligaments`.
	· A fold of peritoneum or other membrane
	· The remnants of a tubular structure from the fetal period of life The first meaning is most commonly what is meant by the term `Ligament`
Lordosis	Lordosis is a medical term used to describe an inward curvature of a portion of the vertebral column. Two segments of the vertebral column, namely cervical and lumbar, are normally lordotic, that is, they are set in a curve that has its convexity anteriorly (the front) and concavity posteriorly (behind), in the context of human anatomy. When referring to the anatomy of other mammals, the direction of the curve is termed ventral.
Lumbar vertebrae	The Lumbar vertebrae are the largest segments of the movable part of the vertebral column, and are characterized by the absence of the foramen transversarium within the transverse process, and by the absence of facets on the sides of the body. They are designated L1 to L5, starting at the top.
	These are the general characteristics of the first through fourth Lumbar vertebrae.

Chapter 1. PART I: Chapter 1 - Chapter 4

Lymphatic system	The Lymphatic system in vertebrates is a network of conduits that carry a clear fluid called lymph. It also includes the lymphoid tissue through which the lymph travels. Lymphoid tissue is found in many organs, particularly the lymph nodes, and in the lymphoid follicles associated with the digestive system such as the tonsils.
Mandible	The Mandible or inferior maxillary bone forms the lower jaw and holds the lower teeth in place. It also refers to both the upper and lower sections of the beaks of birds; in this case the `lower Mandible` corresponds to the Mandible of humans while the `upper Mandible` is functionally equivalent to the human maxilla but mainly consists of the premaxillary bones. Conversely, in bony fish for example, the Mandible may be termed `lower maxilla`. The Mandible consists of: · a curved, horizontal portion, the body.
Osteoarthritis	Osteoarthritis (OA, also known as degenerative arthritis, degenerative joint disease), is a group of diseases and mechanical abnormalities entailing degradation of joints, including articular cartilage and the subchondral bone next to it. Clinical symptoms of OA may include joint pain, tenderness, stiffness, inflammation, creaking, and locking of joints. In OA, a variety of potential forces--hereditary, developmental, metabolic, and mechanical--may initiate processes leading to loss of cartilage -- a strong protein matrix that lubricates and cushions the joints.
Osteotomy	An Osteotomy is a surgical operation whereby a bone is cut to shorten, lengthen, or change its alignment. It is sometimes performed to correct a hallux valgus, or to straighten a bone that has healed crookedly following a fracture. It is also used to correct a coxa vara, genu valgum, and genu varum.
Percutaneous	In surgery, Percutaneous pertains to any medical procedure where access to inner organs or other tissue is done via needle-puncture of the skin, rather than by using an `open` approach where inner organs or tissue are exposed (typically with the use of a scalpel). The Percutaneous approach is commonly used in vascular procedures. This involves a needle catheter getting access to a blood vessel, followed by the introduction of a wire through the lumen of the needle.

Chapter 1. PART I: Chapter 1 - Chapter 4

Scoliosis	Scoliosis is a medical condition in which a person's spine is curved from side to side. Although, it is a complex three-dimensional deformity, on an x-ray, viewed from the rear, the spine of an individual with a typical Scoliosis may look more like an `S` or a `C` than a straight line. It is typically classified as either congenital , idiopathic (cause unknown, sub-classified as infantile, juvenile, adolescent, or adult according to when onset occurred) or neuromuscular (having developed as a secondary symptom of another condition, such as spina bifida, cerebral palsy, spinal muscular atrophy or physical trauma).
Spondylitis	Spondylitis is an inflammation of a vertebra. Any disorder of the spinal column may be called spondylopathy, also.
	Pott's disease is tuberculous disease of the vertebrae marked by stiffness of the vertebral column, pain on motion, tenderness on pressure, prominence of certain of the vertebral spines, and occasionally abdominal pain, abscess formation, and paralysis.
Sublingual gland	The Sublingual glands are salivary glands in the mouth.
	They lie anterior to the submandibular gland under the tongue, beneath the mucous membrane of the floor of the mouth.
	They are drained by 8-20 excretory ducts called the ducts of Rivinus.
Subluxation	A Subluxation may have different meanings, depending on the medical specialty involved. It implies the presence of an incomplete or partial dislocation of a joint or organ. The World Health Organization (WHO) defines both the medical Subluxation and the chiropractic Subluxation.
Trigone	Trigone can refer to: · Trigone of urinary bladder · Fibrous Trigone · Olfactory Trigone

---

	· Trigone of the lateral ventricle `
Cecum	The Cecum or caecum is a pouch, connecting the ileum with the ascending colon of the large intestine. It is separated from the ileum by the ileocecal valve or Bauhin's valve, and is considered to be the beginning of the large intestine. It is also separated from the colon by the cecocolic junction.
Respiratory tract	In humans the Respiratory tract is the part of the anatomy that has to do with the process of respiration.
	The Respiratory tract is divided into 3 segments:
	· Upper Respiratory tract: nose and nasal passages, paranasal sinuses, and throat or pharynx
	· Respiratory airways: voice box or larynx, trachea, bronchi, and bronchioles
	· Lungs: respiratory bronchioles, alveolar ducts, alveolar sacs, and alveoli The Respiratory tract is a common site for infections. Upper Respiratory tract infections are probably the most common infections in the world.
	Most of the Respiratory tract exists merely as a piping system for air to travel in the lungs; alveoli are the only part of the lung that exchanges oxygen and carbon dioxide with the blood.
Osteomyelitis	Osteomyelitis simply means an infection of the bone or bone marrow. It can be usefully subclassified on the basis of the causative organism , the route, duration and anatomic location of the infection.
	In general, microorganisms may infect bone through one or more of three basic methods: via the bloodstream, contiguously from local areas of infection (as in cellulitis), or penetrating trauma, including iatrogenic causes such as joint replacements or internal fixation of fractures or root-canaled teeth.

Chapter 1. PART I: Chapter 1 - Chapter 4

Osteoporosis	Osteoporosis is a disease of bone that leads to an increased risk of fracture. In osteoporosis the bone mineral density (BMD) is reduced, bone microarchitecture is disrupted, and the amount and variety of proteins in bone is altered. osteoporosis is defined by the World Health Organization (WHO) in women as a bone mineral density 2.5 standard deviations below peak bone mass (20-year-old healthy female average) as measured by DXA; the term `established osteoporosis` includes the presence of a fragility fracture.
Sprain	A Sprain is an injury to ligaments that is caused by being stretched beyond their normal capacity and possibly torn. A muscular tear caused in the same manner is referred to as a strain. In cases where either ligament or muscle tissue is torn, immobilization and surgical repair may be necessary.
Strain	Strain can refer to: · Strain a variant of a plant, virus or bacterium; or an inbred animal used for experimental purposes · Strain a chemical stress of a molecule · Strain geometrical measure of deformation representing the relative displacement between particles in a material body, i.e. a measure of how much a given displacement differs locally from a rigid-body displacement. · Strain an injury to a muscle in which the muscle fibers tear as a result of over stretching · Strain manga written by Yoshiyuki Okamura, and illustrated by Ryoichi Ikegami · Strain a series of musical phrases that create a distinct melody of a piece · Christina Strain, a comic book artist (colorist) · Isaac Strain, an American explorer · Julie Strain, an American actress and model .
Arthritis	Arthritis is a group of conditions involving damage to the joints of the body.

	There are over 100 different forms of Arthritis. The most common form, osteoArthritis is a result of trauma to the joint, infection of the joint, or age.
Osteomalacia	Osteomalacia term for the softening of the bones due to defective bone mineralization. Osteomalacia in children is known as rickets, and because of this, use of the term Osteomalacia is often restricted to the milder, adult form of the disease. It may show signs as diffuse body pains, muscle weakness, and fragility of the bones.
Rickets	Rickets is a softening of bones in children potentially leading to fractures and deformity. Rickets is among the most frequent childhood diseases in many developing countries. The predominant cause is a vitamin D deficiency, but lack of adequate calcium in the diet may also lead to Rickets (cases of severe diarrhea and vomiting may be the cause of the deficiency).
Spina bifida	Spina bifida is a developmental birth defect caused by the incomplete closure of the embryonic neural tube. Some vertebrae overlying the spinal cord are not fully formed and remain unfused and open. If the opening is large enough, this allows a portion of the spinal cord to stick out through the opening in the bones.
Ankylosing spondylitis	Ankylosing spondylitis, previously known as Bechterew's disease, Bechterew syndrome, and Marie Strümpell disease, a form of Spondyloarthritis, is a chronic, inflammatory arthritis and autoimmune disease. It mainly affects joints in the spine and the sacroilium in the pelvis, and can cause eventual fusion of the spine. It is a member of the group of the spondyloarthropathies with a strong genetic predisposition.
Gout	Gout is a disease hallmarked by elevated levels of uric acid in the bloodstream. In this condition, crystals of monosodium urate (MSU) or uric acid are deposited on the articular cartilage of joints, tendons, and surrounding tissues.[546] It is marked by transient painful attacks of acute arthritis initiated by crystallization of urates within and about the joints and can eventually lead to chronic Gouty arthritis and the deposition of masses of urates in joints and other sites, sometimes creating tophi. Historically, it was known as `The Disease of Kings` or `Rich man`s disease`.

Chapter 1. PART I: Chapter 1 - Chapter 4

Rheumatoid arthritis	Rheumatoid arthritis is a chronic, systemic inflammatory disorder that may affect many tissues and organs, but principally attacks the joints producing an inflammatory synovitis that often progresses to destruction of the articular cartilage and ankylosis of the joints. Rheumatoid arthritis can also produce diffuse inflammation in the lungs, pericardium, pleura, and sclera, and also nodular lesions, most common in subcutaneous tissue under the skin. Although the cause of Rheumatoid arthritis is unknown, autoimmunity plays a pivotal role in its chronicity and progression.
Septic arthritis	Septic arthritis is the purulent invasion of a joint by an infectious agent which produces arthritis. The term `suppurative arthritis` is a near synonym for Septic arthritis. (`Suppurative` refers to the production of pus, without necessarily implying sepsis).
Bone tumor	A Bone tumor refers to a neoplastic growth of tissue in bone. It can be used for both benign and malignant abnormal growths found in bone, but is most commonly used for primary tumors of bone, such as osteosarcoma. It is may be applied to secondary Bone tumors, i.e. metastatic tumors found in bone.
Chondroblastoma	Chondroblastoma is a rare bone tumor, usually benign with a slow-growing nature. In children, it is the most common epiphyseal tumor. It originates from chondroblasts, hence the name.
Muscular dystrophy	Muscular dystrophy refers to a group of genetic, hereditary muscle diseases that weaken the muscles that move the human body. Muscular dystrophies are characterized by progressive skeletal muscle weakness, defects in muscle proteins, and the death of muscle cells and tissue. Nine diseases including Duchenne, Becker, limb girdle, congenital, facioscapulohumeral, myotonic, oculopharyngeal, distal, and Emery-Dreifuss are always classified as Muscular dystrophy but there are more than 100 diseases in total with similarities to Muscular dystrophy.
Osteosarcoma	Osteosarcoma is the most common type of malignant bone cancer, accounting for 35% of primary bone malignancies. There is a preference for the metaphyseal region of tubular long bones. 50% of cases occur around the knee.

Chapter 1. PART I: Chapter 1 - Chapter 4

Polymyositis	Polymyositis is a type of chronic inflammatory myopathy related to dermatomyositis and inclusion body myositis. Polymyositis means `many muscle inflammation`. Polymyositis tends to become evident in adulthood, presenting with bilateral proximal muscle weakness often noted in the upper legs due to early fatigue while walking.
Dystrophy	Dystrophy is any condition of abnormal development, often denoting the degeneration of muscles. · Muscular dystrophy · Duchenne muscular dystrophy · Becker`s muscular dystrophy · Reflex sympathetic dystrophy · Retinal dystrophy · Conal dystrophy · Myotonic dystrophy · Corneal dystrophies .
Fibromyalgia	Fibromyalgia (new lat., fibro-, fibrous tissue, Gk. myo-, muscle, Gk. algos-, pain), meaning muscle and connective tissue pain (also referred to as FM or FMS), is a medically unexplained syndrome characterized by chronic widespread pain and a heightened and painful response to pressure (allodynia).
Tumor	A tumor or tumour is the name for a swelling or lesion formed by an abnormal growth of cells (termed neoplastic). tumor is not synonymous with cancer. A tumor can be benign, pre-malignant or malignant, whereas cancer is by definition malignant.
Multiple myeloma	Multiple myeloma , also known as Multiple myeloma, myeloma, plasma cell myeloma,) is a cancer of the white blood cells known as plasma cells, which produce antibodies.

	These plasma cells, or B cells, are part of the immune system, formed in bone marrow, and numerous in lymphatics. Myeloma is incurable, but remissions may be induced with steroids, chemotherapy, thalidomide and stem cell transplants.
Larynx	The Larynx , colloquially known as the `voice box`, is an organ in the neck of mammals involved in protection of the trachea and sound production. It manipulates pitch and volume. The Larynx houses the vocal folds, which are an essential component of phonation.
Pharynx	The pharynx is the part of the neck and throat situated immediately posterior to the mouth and nasal cavity, and cranial, or superior, to the esophagus, larynx, and trachea. The pharynx is part of the digestive system and respiratory system of many organisms. Because both food and air pass through the pharynx, a flap of connective tissue called the epiglottis closes over the trachea when food is swallowed to prevent choking or aspiration.
Respiratory system	The respiratory system`s function is to allow gas exchange to all parts of the body. The space between the alveoli and the capillaries, the anatomy or structure of the exchange system, and the precise physiological uses of the exchanged gases vary depending on the organism. In humans and other mammals, for example, the anatomical features of the respiratory system include airways, lungs, and the respiratory muscles.
Upper respiratory tract	The upper respiratory tract refers to the following parts of the respiratory system: · nose and paranasal sinuses · oral cavity (also part of the digestive system) · throat · pharynx · nasopharynx

· oropharynx

· laryngopharynx

· larynx (The larynx can be considered part of the upper respiratory tract or the lower respiratory tract depending on the source. Some specify that the glottis (vocal cords) is the defining line between the upper and lower respiratory tracts; others make the line at the cricoid cartilage). upper respiratory tract infections are amongst the most common infections in the world.

Voice box	Voice box could mean: · The larynx , colloquially known as the voicebox, is an organ in the neck of mammals involved in protection of the trachea and sound production. · The Talk box, a musical sound effects device that allows a musician to modify the sound of a musical instrument by changing the shape of the mouth. · The Mechanical larynx, used by people who have lost their voicebox due to disease or smoking-associated ailments. · VoiceBox Technologies, a company focused on speech recognition, and voice search.
Family	Family is a group of people or animals (many species form the equivalent of a human Family wherein the adults care for the young) affiliated by consanguinity, affinity or co-residence. Although the concept of consanguinity originally referred to relations by `blood`, anthropologists have argued that one must understand the idea of `blood` metaphorically and that many societies understand Family through other concepts rather than through genetic distance. One of the primary functions of the Family is to produce and reproduce persons, biologically and socially.
Regurgitation	Regurgitation, Regurgiate or Regurgitate can refer to:

· Regurgitation

· Vomiting

· Regurgitation

· Regurgitate (band), a goregrind band `

Alveolar duct

Alveolar ducts are the tiny end ducts of the branching airways that fill the lungs. Each lung holds approximately 1.5 to 2 million of them. The tubules divide into two or three alveolar sacs at the distal end.

Bronchiole

The Bronchioles or bronchioli are the first airway branches that no longer contain cartilage. They are branches of the bronchi. The Bronchioles terminate by entering the circular sacs called alveoli.

Sclerosis

Sclerosis or sclerotization is a hardening of tissue and other anatomical features;

· Sclerosis

· Cyberbrain Sclerosis, a fictional disease introduced in Ghost in the Shell: Stand Alone Complex. The disease is characterized by hardening of the brain tissues precipitated by the cyberization process.

· a process which hardens plant tissue by adding fibers and sclereids, resulting in sclerenchyma

Lung

The Lung or pulmonary system is the essential respiration organ in air-breathing animals, including most tetrapods, a few fish and a few snails. In mammals and the more complex life forms, the two Lungs are located in the chest on either side of the heart. Their principal function is to transport oxygen from the atmosphere into the bloodstream, and to release carbon dioxide from the bloodstream into the atmosphere.

Adenoidectomy

Adenoidectomy is the surgical removal of the adenoids. They may be removed for several reasons, including impaired breathing through the nose and chronic infections or earaches. The surgery is common.

Cram101

Chapter 1. PART I: Chapter 1 - Chapter 4

Apnea	Apnea, apnoea, or apnÅ"a is a term for suspension of external breathing. During Apnea there is no movement of the muscles of respiration and the volume of the lungs initially remains unchanged. Depending on the patency (openness) of the airways there may or may not be a flow of gas between the lungs and the environment; gas exchange within the lungs and cellular respiration is not affected.
Asphyxia	Asphyxia is a condition of severely deficient supply of oxygen to the body that arises from being unable to breathe normally. An example of Asphyxia is choking. Asphyxia causes generalized hypoxia, which primarily affects the tissues and organs.
Asthma	Asthma is a common chronic inflammatory disease of the airways characterized by variable and recurring symptoms, airflow obstruction, and bronchospasm. Symptoms include wheezing, cough, chest tightness, and shortness of breath. Medicines such as inhaled short-acting beta-2 agonists may be used to treat acute attacks.
Atelectasis	Atelectasis is a medical condition in which the lungs are not fully inflated. It may affect part or all of one lung. It is a condition where the alveoli are deflated, as distinct from pulmonary consolidation.
Auscultation	Auscultation is the technical term for listening to the internal sounds of the body, usually using a stethoscope; based on the Latin verb auscultare 'to listen'. Auscultation is performed for the purposes of examining the circulatory system and respiratory system , as well as the gastrointestinal system (bowel sounds). The term was introduced by René-Théophile-Hyacinthe Laennec.
Bacilli	Bacilli refers to a taxonomic class of bacteria. It includes two orders, Bacillales and Lactobacillales, which contain several well-known pathogens like Bacillus anthracis (the cause of anthrax). There are several related concepts that make use of similar words, and the ambiguity can create considerable confusion.

Bronchoscopy	Bronchoscopy is a technique of visualizing the inside of the airways for diagnostic and therapeutic purposes. An instrument (bronchoscope) is inserted into the airways, usually through the nose or mouth, or occasionally through a tracheostomy. This allows the practitioner to examine the patient's airways for abnormalities such as foreign bodies, bleeding, tumors, or inflammation.
Catheter	In medicine a Catheter is a tube that can be inserted into a body cavity, duct or vessel. Catheters thereby allow drainage, injection of fluids or access by surgical instruments. The process of inserting a Catheter is Catheterization.
Cauterization	The medical practice or technique of cauterization is a medical term describing the burning of part of a body to remove or close off a part of it in a process called cautery, which destroys some tissue, in an attempt to mitigate damage, remove an undesired growth, or minimize other potential medical harmful possibilities such as infections, when antibiotics are not available. The practice was once widespread and is still used in remote regions of the world such as central Australia for treatment of wounds. Its utility before the advent of antibiotics was effective on several levels: · useful in stopping severe blood-loss, · to close amputations, · useful in preventing infections, including complications from septicaemia. Actual cautery is a term referring to the white-hot iron--a metal generally heated only up to a dull red glow--that is applied to produce blisters, to stop bleeding of a blood vessel, and other similar purposes.
Cordectomy	Cordectomy is the surgical removal of a cord. It usually refers to removal of the vocal cord, often for the purpose of treating Laryngeal Cancer . It can be carried out by traditional surgical techniques or, increasingly, by Carbon Dioxide Laser .
Croup	Croup is a group of respiratory diseases that often affects infants and children under age 6. It is characterized by a barking cough; a whistling, obstructive sound (stridor) as the child breathes in; and hoarseness due to obstruction in the region of the larynx. It may be mild, moderate or severe, and severe cases, with breathing difficulty, can be fatal if not treated in a hospital.
Cyanosis	Cyanosis is a blue coloration of the skin and mucous membranes due to the presence of > 5g/dl deoxygenated hemoglobin in blood vessels near the skin surface.

Although human blood is always a shade of red (except in rare cases of hemoglobin-related disease), the optical properties of skin distort the dark red color of deoxygenated blood to make it appear bluish.

The elementary principle behind Cyanosis is that deoxygenated hemoglobin is more prone to the optical bluish discoloration, and also produces vasoconstriction that makes it more evident.

Dysphonia	Dysphonia is the medical term for disorders of the voice: an impairment in the ability to produce voice sounds using the vocal organs . Thus, Dysphonia is a phonation disorder. The dysphonic voice can be hoarse or weak, or excessively breathy, harsh, or rough, but some kind of phonation is still possible (contrasted with the more severe aphonia where phonation is impossible).
Dyspnea	Dyspnea or dyspnoea , from Latin dyspnoea, from Greek dyspnoia from dyspnoos, shortness of breath), also called shortness of breath or air hunger, is a debilitating symptom that is the experience of unpleasant or uncomfortable respiratory sensations. It is a common symptom of numerous medical disorders, particularly those involving the cardiovascular and respiratory systems; Dyspnea on exertion is the most common presenting complaint for people with respiratory impairment.

Dyspnea has been more specifically defined by the American Thoracic Society as the `subjective experience of breathing discomfort that consists of qualitatively distinct sensations that vary in intensity. |
Emphysema	Emphysema is a long-term, progressive disease of the lung that primarily causes shortness of breath. In people with Emphysema, the lung tissues necessary to support the physical shape and function of the lung are destroyed. It is included in a group of diseases called chronic obstructive pulmonary disease or COPD (pulmonary refers to the lungs).
Epistaxis	Epistaxis is the relatively common occurrence of hemorrhage from the nose, usually noticed when the blood drains out through the nostrils. There are two types: anterior , and posterior (less common, more likely to require medical attention). Sometimes in more severe cases, the blood can come up the nasolacrimal duct and out from the eye.
Hemoptysis	Hemoptysis or haemoptysis is the expectoration (coughing up) of blood or of blood-stained sputum from the bronchi, larynx, trachea, or lungs (e.g. in tuberculosis or other respiratory infections).

	This can be due to bronchitis or pneumonia most commonly, but also to lung neoplasm (in smokers, when Hemoptysis is persistent), aspergilloma, tuberculosis, bronchiectasis, coccidioidomycosis, pulmonary embolism, or pneumonic plague.
	Rarer causes include hereditary hemorrhagic telangiectasia (HHT or Rendu-Osler-Weber syndrome), or Goodpasture`s syndrome and Wegener`s granulomatosis.
Intubation	In medicine, Intubation refers to the placement of a tube into an external or internal orifice of the body. Although the term can refer to endoscopic procedures, it is most often used to denote tracheal Intubation. Tracheal Intubation is the placement of a flexible plastic tube into the trachea to protect the patient`s airway and provide a means of mechanical ventilation.
Laryngectomy	Laryngectomy is the removal of the larynx and separation of the airway from the mouth, nose, and esophagus. The laryngectomee breathes through an opening in the neck, a stoma. It is done in cases of laryngeal cancer.
Hypopharynx	In human anatomy, the hypopharynx is the bottom part of the pharynx, and is the part of the throat that connects to the esophagus.
	The superior boundary of the hypopharynx is at the level of the hyoid bone.
	It can be divided into three sites:
	· Pyriform sinus
	· Postcricoid area
	· Posterior pharyngeal wall
Laryngoscope	A Laryngoscope (larynx+scope) is a medical instrument that is used to obtain a view of the vocal folds and the glottis, which is the space between the cords. The first Laryngoscope was invented in 1854 by Manuel Patricio Rodríguez García. There are many types of Laryngoscopes.

Chapter 1. PART I: Chapter 1 - Chapter 4

Laryngotomy	Laryngotomy is the surgical operation of cutting into the larynx, possibly with specialized equipment such as a laryngotome. The surgical creation of a permanent opening in the larynx is referred to as laryngostomy. Laryngotomy is an important procedure in assisting respiration when the upper part of the airway has been obstructed. · For inferior Laryngotomy or emergency Laryngotomy, see Cricothyrotomy. · For median Laryngotomy involving cutting of the thyroid cartilage, see Thyroidotomy.
Lavage	In medicine, Lavage is a general term referring to cleaning or rinsing. Specific types include: · Antiseptic Lavage · Bronchoalveolar Lavage · Gastric Lavage · Peritoneal Lavage · Arthroscopic Lavage · Ductal Lavage · Ear Lavage The French noun Lavage was imported intact into medical English. This explains the French-like pronunciation. However, the word has been more or less naturalized, which explains the naturalized variant pronunciation.
Oropharynx	The Oropharynx reaches from the Uvula to the level of the hyoid bone.

It opens anteriorly, through the isthmus faucium, into the mouth, while in its lateral wall, between the two palatine arches, is the palatine tonsil.

Although older resources have stated that Fusobacterium is a common occurrence in the human Oropharynx, the current consensus is that Fusobacterium should always be treated as a pathogen.

The name is formed from their initials:

· Haemophilus

· Actinobacillus actinomycetemcomitans

· Cardiobacterium hominis

· Eikenella corrodens

· Kingella

All of these organisms are part of the normal oropharyngeal flora which grow slowly, prefer a carbon dioxide-enriched atmosphere and share an enhanced capacity to produce endocardial infections, especially in young children.

Orthopnea	Orthopnea or orthopnoea is shortness of breath which occurs when lying flat, causing the person to have to sleep propped up in bed or sitting in a chair. It is the opposite of platypnea.
	It is commonly measured according to the number of pillows needed to prop the patient up to enable breathing (Example: `3 pillow Orthopnea`).
Percussion	A Percussion instrument is any object which produces a sound by being hit with an implement, shaken, rubbed, scraped, or by any other action which sets the object into vibration. The term usually applies to an object used in a rhythmic context or with musical intent.
	The word `Percussion` has evolved from Latin terms: `percussio`, and `percussus` (which is a noun meaning `a beating`).

Chapter 1. PART I: Chapter 1 - Chapter 4

Pertussis	Pertussis, also known as the whooping cough, is a highly contagious disease caused by the bacterium Bordetella Pertussis. It derived its name from the `whoop` sound made from the inspiration of air after a cough. A similar, milder disease is caused by B. paraPertussis.
Pleura	In human anatomy, the Pleural cavity is the body cavity that surrounds the lungs. The Pleura is a serous membrane which folds back upon itself to form a two-layered, membrane structure. The thin space between the two Pleural layers is known as the Pleural cavity; it normally contains a small amount of Pleural fluid.
Pneumonia	Pneumonia is an inflammatory illness of the lung. Frequently, it is described as lung parenchyma/alveolar inflammation and abnormal alveolar filling with fluid (consolidation and exudation). The alveoli are microscopic air-filled sacs in the lungs responsible for absorbing oxygen.
Pulmonary edema	Pulmonary edema is fluid accumulation in the lungs. It leads to impaired gas exchange and may cause respiratory failure. It is due to either failure of the heart to remove fluid from the lung circulation (`cardiogenic Pulmonary edema`) or a direct injury to the lung parenchyma (`noncardiogenic Pulmonary edema`).
Pulmonary embolism	Pulmonary embolism is a blockage of the main artery of the lung or one of its branches by a substance that has travelled from elsewhere in the body through the bloodstream (embolism). Usually this is due to embolism of a thrombus (blood clot) from the deep veins in the legs, a process termed venous thromboembolism. A small proportion is due to the embolization of air, fat or amniotic fluid.
Rales	Rales, crackles or crepitations, are the clicking, rattling, or crackling noises heard on auscultation of the lung with a stethoscope during inhalation. Crackles are caused by the `popping open` of small airways and alveoli collapsed by fluid, exudate, or lack of aeration during expiration. The word `Rales` derives from the French word râle meaning `rattle`.
Embolism	In medicine, an Embolism (plural Embolisms) occurs when an object migrates from one part of the body (through circulation) and causes a blockage (occlusion) of a blood vessel in another part of the body. The term was coined in 1848 by Rudolph Carl Virchow. This is in contrast with a thrombus, or clot, which forms at the blockage point within a blood vessel and is not carried from somewhere else.

97

Chapter 1. PART I: Chapter 1 - Chapter 4

Rhinoplasty	Rhinoplasty is a surgical procedure which is usually performed by either an otolaryngologist-head and neck surgeon, maxillofacial surgeon,) of a human nose. Rhinoplasty is also commonly called `nose reshaping` or `nose job`. Rhinoplasty can be performed to meet aesthetic goals or for reconstructive purposes to correct trauma, birth defects or breathing problems.
Rhinorrhea	Rhinorrhea, commonly referred to as runny nose, consists of an unusually significant amount of nasal fluid. It is a symptom of the common cold and of allergies (hay fever). The term is a combination of the Greek words `rhinos` meaning `of the nose` and `-rrhea` meaning `discharge or flow`.
Sarcoidosis	Sarcoidosis is a systemic disease of unknown aetiology that results in the formation of non-caseating granulomas in multiple organs. The prevalence is higher among blacks than whites by a ratio of 20:1. Usually the disease is localized to the chest, but urogenital involvement is found in 0.2% of clinically diagnosed cases and 5% of those diagnosed at necropsy.
Septoplasty	Septoplasty is a corrective surgical procedure done to straighten the nasal septum, the partition between the two nasal cavities. Ideally, the septum should run down the center of the nose. When it deviates into one of the cavities, it narrows that cavity and impedes airflow.
Spirometry	Spirometry (meaning the measuring of breath) is the most common of the Pulmonary Function Tests (PFTs), measuring lung function, specifically the measurement of the amount (volume) and/or speed (flow) of air that can be inhaled and exhaled. Spirometry is an important tool used for generating pneumotachographs which are helpful in assessing conditions such as asthma, pulmonary fibrosis, cystic fibrosis, and COPD. Device for Spirometry. The patient places his or her lips around the blue mouthpiece.
Tachypnea	Tachypnea is characterized by rapid breathing. It is not identical with hyperventilation - Tachypnea may be necessary for a sufficient gas-exchange of the body, for example after exercise, in which case it is not hyperventilation. Tachypnea differs from hyperpnea in that Tachypnea is rapid shallow breaths, while hyperpnea is rapid deep breaths.

Chapter 1. PART I: Chapter 1 - Chapter 4

Thoracic vertebrae	In the human 12 Thoracic vertebrae compose the middle segment of the vertebral column, between the cervical vertebrae and the lumbar vertebrae. They are intermediate in size between those of the cervical and lumbar regions; they increase in size as one proceeds down the spine, the upper vertebrae being much smaller than those in the lower part of the region. They are distinguished by the presence of facets on the sides of the bodies for articulation with the heads of the ribs, and facets on the transverse processes of all, except the eleventh and twelfth, for articulation with the tubercles of the ribs.
Thoracoscopy	Thoracoscopy is a medical procedure involving internal inspection of the pleural cavity. It was developed by Hans Christian Jacobaeus, a Swedish internist in 1910 for the treatment of tuberculous intra-thoracic adhesions. He used a cystoscope to examine the thoracic cavity, developing his technique over the next twenty years.
Thoracotomy	Thoracotomy is an incision into the pleural space of the chest. It is performed by a surgeon, and, rarely, by emergency physicians, to gain access to the thoracic organs, most commonly the heart, the lungs, the esophagus or thoracic aorta, or for access to the anterior spine such as is necessary for access to tumors in the spine. Thoracotomy is a major surgical maneuver--the first step in many thoracic surgeries including lobectomy or pneumonectomy for lung cancer--and as such requires general anesthesia with endotracheal tube insertion and mechanical ventilation.
Thyroid-stimulating hormone	Thyroid-stimulating hormone is a peptide hormone synthesized and secreted by thyrotrope cells in the anterior pituitary gland, which regulates the endocrine function of the thyroid gland. TSH stimulates the thyroid gland to secrete the hormones thyroxine and triiodothyronine (T_3). TSH production is controlled by thyrotropin-releasing hormone (TRH), which is manufactured in the hypothalamus and transported to the anterior pituitary gland via the superior hypophyseal artery, where it increases TSH production and release.
Tracheostomy	Tracheotomy and Tracheostomy are surgical procedures on the neck to open a direct airway through an incision in the trachea (the windpipe). They are performed by paramedics, veterinarians, emergency physicians and surgeons. Both surgical and percutaneous techniques are now widely used.

Chapter 1. PART I: Chapter 1 - Chapter 4

Tracheotomy	Tracheotomy and tracheostomy are surgical procedures on the neck to open a direct airway through an incision in the trachea (the windpipe). They are performed by paramedics, veterinarians, emergency physicians and surgeons. Both surgical and percutaneous techniques are now widely used.
Tuberculosis	Tuberculosis or TB (short for Tubercle Bacillus) is a common and often deadly infectious disease caused by mycobacteria, usually Mycobacterium Tuberculosis in humans. Tuberculosis usually attacks the lungs but can also affect other parts of the body. It is spread through the air, when people who have the disease cough, sneeze, or spit.
Pneumonectomy	A Pneumonectomy is a surgical procedure to remove a lung. Removal of just one lobe of the lung is specifically referred to as a lobectomy, and that of a segment of the lung as a wedge resection (or segmentectomy). The most common reason for a Pneumonectomy is to remove tumourous tissue arising from lung cancer.
Costal cartilage	The Costal cartilages are bars of hyaline cartilage which serve to prolong the ribs forward and contribute very materially to the elasticity of the walls of the thorax. The first seven pairs are connected with the sternum; the next three are each articulated with the lower border of the cartilage of the preceding rib; the last two have pointed extremities, which end in the wall of the abdomen. Like the ribs, the Costal cartilages vary in their length, breadth, and direction.
Cough	A Cough (Â·) Latin: tussis), in medicine, is a sudden and often repetitively occurring defense reflex which helps to clear the large breathing passages from excess secretions, irritants, foreign particles and microbes. The Cough reflex consists of three phases: an inhalation, a forced exhalation against a closed glottis, and a violent release of air from the lungs following opening of the glottis, usually accompanied by a distinctive sound. Coughing can happen voluntarily as well as involuntarily, though for the most part, involuntarily.
Hypercapnia	Hypercapnia or hypercapnea , also known as hypercarbia, is a condition where there is too much carbon dioxide in the blood. Carbon dioxide is a gaseous product of the body's metabolism and is normally expelled through the lungs.

	Hypercapnia normally triggers a reflex which increases breathing and access to oxygen, such as arousal and turning the head during sleep.
Hyperventilation	In medicine, Hyperventilation is the state of breathing faster and/or deeper than necessary, bringing about lightheadedness and other undesirable symptoms often associated with panic attacks. Hyperventilation can also be a response to metabolic acidosis, a condition that causes acidic blood pH levels. Counterintuitively, such side effects are not precipitated by the sufferer's lack of oxygen or air.
Hypoventilation	In medicine, Hypoventilation (also known as respiratory depression) occurs when ventilation is inadequate (hypo means 'below') to perform needed gas exchange. By definition it causes an increased concentration of carbon dioxide (hypercapnia) and respiratory acidosis. It can be caused by medical conditions, such as stroke affecting the brain stem, by holding one's breath, or by drugs, typically when taken in overdose.
Hypoxemia	Hypoxemia is generally defined as decreased partial pressure of oxygen in blood, sometimes specifically as less than 60 mmHg (8.0 kPa) or causing hemoglobin oxygen saturation of less than 90%. The Hypoxemia definition as decreased partial pressure of oxygen excludes decreased oxygen content caused by anemia (decreased content of oxygen binding protein hemoglobin) or other primary hemoglobin deficiency, because they don't decrease the partial pressure of oxygen in blood. Still, some simply define it as insufficient oxygenation or total oxygen content of (arterial) blood, which, without further specification, would include both concentration of dissolved oxygen and oxygen bound to hemoglobin.
Pulmonary arteries	The pulmonary arteries carry blood from heart to the lungs. They are the only arteries (other than umbilical arteries in the fetus) that carry deoxygenated blood. In the human heart, the pulmonary trunk (pulmonary artery or main pulmonary artery) begins at the base of the right ventricle.

Chapter 1. PART I: Chapter 1 - Chapter 4

Cartilage	Cartilage is a stiff yet flexible connective tissue found in many areas in the bodies of humans and other animals, including the joints between bones, the rib cage, the ear, the nose, the elbow, the knee, the ankle, the bronchial tubes and the intervertebral discs. It is not as hard and rigid as bone but is stiffer and less flexible than muscle.
	Cartilage is composed of specialized cells called chondrocytes that produce a large amount of extracellular matrix composed of collagen fibers, abundant ground substance rich in proteoglycan, and elastin fibers.
Respiratory failure	The term Respiratory failure, in medicine, is used to describe inadequate gas exchange by the respiratory system, with the result that arterial oxygen and/or carbon dioxide levels cannot be maintained within their normal ranges. A drop in blood oxygenation is known as hypoxemia; a rise in arterial carbon dioxide levels is called hypercapnia. The normal reference values are: oxygen $PaO_2 > 60$ mmHg, and carbon dioxide PaCO2 < 45 mmHg.
Bronchiectasis	Bronchiectasis is a disease state defined by localized, irreversible dilation of part of the bronchial tree. It is classified as an obstructive lung disease, along with bronchitis and cystic fibrosis. Involved bronchi are dilated, inflamed, and easily collapsible, resulting in airflow obstruction and impaired clearance of secretions.
Bronchiolitis	Bronchiolitis is inflammation of the bronchioles, the smallest air passages of the lungs. This inflammation is usually caused by viruses. The term usually refers to acute viral Bronchiolitis, a common disease in infancy.
Respiratory acidosis	Respiratory acidosis is a medical condition in which decreased respiration (hypoventilation) causes increased blood carbon dioxide and decreased pH (a condition generally called acidosis).
	Carbon dioxide is produced constantly as the body burns energy, and this CO_2 will accumulate rapidly if the lungs do not adequately dispel it through alveolar ventilation. Alveolar hypoventilation thus leads to an increased $PaCO_2$ (called hypercapnia).
Acidosis	Acidosis is an increased acidity (i.e. an increased hydrogen ion concentration). If not further qualified, it usually refers to acidity of the blood plasma. Acidosis is said to occur when arterial pH falls below 7.35, while its counterpart (alkalosis) occurs at a pH over 7.45.

Chapter 1. PART I: Chapter 1 - Chapter 4

Cor pulmonale	Cor pulmonale or pulmonary heart disease is a change in structure and function of the right ventricle of the heart as a result of a respiratory disorder. Right ventricular hypertrophy (RVH) is the predominant change in chronic Cor pulmonale, whereas in acute cases, dilation dominates. Both hypertrophy and dilation are the result of increased right ventricular pressure.
Empyema	An Empyema is a collection of pus within a naturally existing anatomical cavity, such as the lung pleura. It must be differentiated from an abscess, which is a collection of pus in a newly formed cavity. Usually an Empyema starts with pneumonia, followed by a parapneumonic effusion.
Exudate	An Exudate is any fluid that filters from the circulatory system into lesions or areas of inflammation. It can apply to plants as well as animals. Its composition varies but generally includes water and the dissolved solutes of the main circulatory fluid such as sap or blood.
Hemothorax	A Hemothorax is a condition that results from blood accumulating in the pleural cavity. Its cause is usually traumatic, from a blunt or penetrating injury to the thorax, resulting in a rupture of the serous membrane either lining the thorax or covering the lungs. This rupture allows blood to spill into the pleural space, equalizing the pressures between it and the lungs.
Pleurisy	Pleurisy, also known as pleuritis, is an inflammation of the pleura, the lining of the pleural cavity surrounding the lungs. Among other things, infections are the most common cause of Pleurisy. The inflamed pleural layers rub against each other every time the lungs expand to breathe in air.
Pneumoconiosis	Pneumoconiosis is an occupational lung disease caused by the inhalation of dust. Depending on the type of dust, variants of the disease are considered. Types include: · Anthracosis - carbon dust · Coalworker's Pneumoconiosis (also known as `black lung`) - coal dust · Asbestosis - asbestos dust

· Silicosis (also known as `grinder`s disease`) - silica dust

· Bauxite fibrosis - bauxite dust

· Berylliosis - beryllium dust

· Siderosis - iron dust

· Byssinosis - cotton dust

· Silicosiderosis - mixed dust containing silica and iron

· Labrador Lung (found in miners in Labrador, Canada) - mixed dust containing iron, silica and anthophyllite, a type of asbestos
Positive indications on patient assessment:

· Shortness of breath

· Chest X-ray may show a characteristic patchy, subpleural, bibasilar interstitial infiltrates or small cystic radiolucencies called honeycombing
Pneumoconiosis in combination with multiple pulmonary rheumatoid nodules in rheumatoid arthritis patients is known as Caplan`s syndrome.

| Pneumothorax | In medicine (pulmonology), a Pneumothorax is a potential medical emergency wherein air or gas is present in the pleural cavity. A Pneumothorax can occur spontaneously. It can also occur as the result of disease or injury to the lung, or due to a puncture to the chest wall. |
| Premenstrual syndrome | Premenstrual syndrome (PMS) is a collection of physical, psychological, and emotional symptoms related to a woman`s menstrual cycle. While most women (about 80 percent) of child-bearing age have some symptoms of PMS, the official definition limits the scope to having symptoms of `sufficient severity to interfere with some aspects of life`. Such symptoms are usually predictable and occur regularly during the two weeks prior to menses. |

Chapter 1. PART I: Chapter 1 - Chapter 4

Chronic obstructive pulmonary disease	Chronic obstructive pulmonary disease refers to chronic bronchitis and emphysema, a pair of two commonly co-existing diseases of the lungs in which the airways become narrowed. This leads to a limitation of the flow of air to and from the lungs causing shortness of breath. In contrast to asthma, the limitation of airflow is poorly reversible and usually gets progressively worse over time.
Chronic bronchitis	Chronic bronchitis is a chronic inflammation of the bronchi (medium-size airways) in the lungs. It is generally considered one of the two forms of chronic obstructive pulmonary disease (COPD). It is defined clinically as a persistent cough that produces sputum (phlegm) and mucus, for at least three months in two consecutive years.
Blood	Blood is a specialized bodily fluid that delivers necessary substances to the body's cells -- such as nutrients and oxygen -- and transports waste products away from those same cells. In vertebrates, it is composed of Blood cells suspended in a liquid called Blood plasma. Plasma, which comprises 55% of Blood fluid, is mostly water (90% by volume), and contains dissolved proteins, glucose, mineral ions, hormones, carbon dioxide (plasma being the main medium for excretory product transportation), platelets and Blood cells themselves.
Blood type	A Blood type is a classification of blood based on the presence or absence of inherited antigenic substances on the surface of red blood cells (RBCs). These antigens may be proteins, carbohydrates, glycoproteins, or glycolipids, depending on the blood group system, and some of these antigens are also present on the surface of other types of cells of various tissues. Several of these red blood cell surface antigens, that stem from one allele (or very closely linked genes), collectively form a blood group system.
Cardiovascular system	The circulatory system is an organ system that passes nutrients (such as amino acids and electrolytes), gases, hormones, blood cells, etc. to and from cells in the body to help fight diseases and help stabilize body temperature and pH to maintain homeostasis. This system may be seen strictly as a blood distribution network, but some consider the circulatory system as composed of the Cardiovascular system, which distributes blood, and the lymphatic system, which distributes lymph.
Platelet	Platelets, or thrombocytes, are small, irregularly-shaped anuclear cells , 2-3 µm in diameter, which are derived from fragmentation of precursor megakaryocytes. The average lifespan of a Platelet is between 8 and 12 days. Platelets play a fundamental role in hemostasis and are a natural source of growth factors.

Cram101

Aorta	The Aorta is the largest artery in the body, originating from the left ventricle of the heart and extends down to the abdomen, where it branches off into two smaller arteries. The Aorta brings oxygenated blood to all parts of the body in the systemic circulation.
	The Aorta is usually divided into five segments/sections:
	· Ascending Aorta--the section between the heart and the arch of Aorta
	· Arch of Aorta--the peak part that looks somewhat like an inverted 'U'
	· Descending Aorta--the section from the arch of Aorta to the point where it divides into the common iliac arteries
	· Thoracic Aorta--the half of the descending Aorta above the diaphragm
	· Abdominal Aorta--the half of the descending Aorta below the diaphragm
	All amniotes have a broadly similar arrangement to that of humans, albeit with a number of individual variations. In fish, however, there are two separate vessels referred to as Aortas.
Glomerulonephritis	Glomerulonephritis, also known as glomerular nephritis, abbreviated GN, is a renal disease characterized by inflammation of the glomeruli, or small blood vessels in the kidneys. It may present with isolated hematuria and/or proteinuria (blood resp. protein in the urine); or as a nephrotic syndrome, a nephritic syndrome, acute renal failure, or chronic renal failure.
Heart	The Heart is a muscular organ found in most vertebrates that is responsible for pumping blood throughout the blood vessels by repeated, rhythmic contractions. The term cardiac (as in cardiology) means `related to the Heart` and comes from the Greek καρδιî¬, kardia, for `Heart.` The vertebrate Heart is composed of cardiac muscle, an involuntary striated muscle tissue which is found only within this organ. The average human Heart, beating at 72 beats per minute, will beat approximately 2.5 billion times during a lifetime (about 66 years).

Chapter 1. PART I: Chapter 1 - Chapter 4

Vein	In the circulatory system, Veins are blood vessels that carry blood towards the heart. Most Veins carry deoxygenated blood from the tissues back to the lungs; exceptions are the pulmonary and umbilical Veins, both of which carry oxygenated blood. They differ from arteries in structure and function; for example, arteries are more muscular than Veins and they carry blood away from the heart.
Interatrial septum	The Interatrial septum is the wall of tissue that separates the right and left atria of the heart.
	The Interatrial septum forms during the first and second months of fetal development. Formation of the septum occurs in several stages.
Interventricular septum	Interventricular septum, abbreviated IVS, is the stout wall separating the lower chambers (the ventricles) of the heart from one another.
	The ventricular septum is directed obliquely backward and to the right, and is curved with the convexity toward the right ventricle: its margins correspond with the anterior and posterior longitudinal sulci.
	· The greater portion of it is thick and muscular and constitutes the muscular ventricular septum.
	· Its upper and posterior part, which separates the aortic vestibule from the lower part of the right atrium and upper part of the right ventricle, is thin and fibrous, and is termed the membranous ventricular septum (septum membranaceum). A hole in the Interventricular septum is termed a ventricular septal defect (VSD).
Septum	In anatomy, a Septum is a wall, dividing a cavity or structure into smaller ones.
	· Interatrial Septum, the wall of tissue that separates the left and right atria of the heart

· Interventricular Septum or median Septum, the wall separating the left and right ventricles of the heart

· Lingual Septum, a vertical layer of fibrous tissue that separates the halves of the tongue

· Nasal Septum: the cartilage wall separating the nostrils of the human nose.

· Alveolar Septum: the thin wall which separates the alveoli from each other.

· Orbital Septum, a palpabral ligament in the upper and lower eyelids

· Septum pellucidum lucidum, a thin structure separating two fluid pockets in the brain

· Uterine Septum, a malformation of the uterus
Histological septa are seen throughout most tissues of the body, particularly where they are needed to stiffen soft cellular tissue, and they also provide planes of ingress for small blood vessels. Because the dense collagen fibres of a Septum usually extend out into the softer adjacent tissues, microscopic fibrous septa are less clearly defined than the macroscopic types of septa listed above. In rare instances, a Septum is a cross-wall.

· One of the radial calcareous plates of a coral. b. One of the transverse partitions dividing the shell of a mollusk, or of a rhizopod, into several chambers. c. One of the transverse partitions dividing the body cavity of an annelid.

· Septum: walls between each chamber, or siphuncle, in shells of nautiloids, ammonites, and belemnites; i.e. cephalopods that retain an external shell.

· A partition dividing filamentous hyphae into discrete cells in fungi

	· A partition that separates the cells of a fruit.
Parenchyma	Parenchyma is a term used to describe a bulk of a substance. It is used in different ways in animals and in plants. The term is New Latin, f.
Pericardial cavity	The Pericardial cavity is a potential space between the parietal pericardium and visceral layer. It contains a supply of serous fluid. The serous fluid that is found in this space is known as the pericardial fluid.
Pericardium	The Pericardium is a double-walled sac that contains the heart and the roots of the great vessels. There are two layers to the pericardial sac: the fibrous Pericardium and the serous Pericardium. The serous Pericardium, in turn, is divided into two layers, the parietal Pericardium, which is fused to and inseparable from the fibrous Pericardium, and the visceral Pericardium, which is part of the epicardium.
Sinoatrial node	The Sinoatrial node is the impulse-generating (pacemaker) tissue located in the right atrium of the heart, and thus the generator of sinus rhythm. It is a group of cells positioned on the wall of the right atrium, near the entrance of the superior vena cava. These cells are modified cardiac myocytes.
Atrioventricular node	The Atrioventricular node is a part of electrical control system of the heart that co-ordinates heart rate. It electrically connects atrial and ventricular chambers. The Atrioventricular node is an area of specialized tissue between the atria and the ventricles of the heart, specifically in the posteroinferior region of the interatrial septum near the opening of the coronary sinus, which conducts the normal electrical impulse from the atria to the ventricles.
Bundle of His	The Bundle of His, also known as the AV bundle or atrioventricular bundle, is a collection of heart muscle cells specialized for electrical conduction that transmits the electrical impulses from the AV node (located between the atria and the ventricles) to the point of the apex of the fascicular branches. The fascicular branches then lead to the Purkinje fibers which innervate the ventricles, causing the cardiac muscle of the ventricles to contract at a paced interval.

Chapter 1. PART I: Chapter 1 - Chapter 4

	These specialized muscle fibres in the heart were named after the Swiss cardiologist Wilhelm His, Jr., who discovered them in 1893.
Diastole	Diastole is the period of time when the heart fills with blood after systole (contraction). Ballistics accurately describes Diastole as recoil opposed to coil or Systole. Ventricular Diastole is the period during which the ventricles are relaxing, while atrial Diastole is the period during which the atria are relaxing.
Acute coronary syndrome	An Acute coronary syndrome is a set of signs and symptoms (syndrome) related to the heart. Acute coronary syndrome is compatible with a diagnosis of acute myocardial ischemia, but it is not characteristic of the diagnosis. The sub-types of Acute coronary syndrome include unstable angina (UA, not associated with heart muscle damage), and two forms of myocardial infarction (MI, heart attack), in which heart muscle is damaged.
Anastomosis	An Anastomosis is a network of streams that both branch out and reconnect, such as blood vessels or leaf veins. The term is used in medicine, biology, mycology and geology.
Angiography	Angiography , or lumen, of blood vessels and organs of the body, with particular interest in the arteries, veins and the heart chambers. This is traditionally done by injecting a radio-opaque contrast agent into the blood vessel and imaging using X-ray based techniques such as fluoroscopy. The word itself comes from the Greek words angeion, 'vessel', and graphein, 'to write or record'.
Angioplasty	Angioplasty is the technique of mechanically widening a narrowed or obstructed blood vessel; typically as a result of atherosclerosis. Tightly folded balloons are passed into the narrowed locations and then inflated to a fixed size using water pressures some 75 to 500 times normal blood pressure (6 to 20 atmospheres). The word is composed of the medical combining forms of the Greek words αγγειος aggeîos meaning 'vessel' and πλαστΪŒς plastós meaning 'formed' or 'moulded'.
Atherectomy	Atherectomy is a minimally invasive method of removing plaque and blockage from an artery in the body and subsequently widening arteries narrowed by arterial disease. Atherectomy falls under the umbrella category of percutaneous revascularization, which refers to a variety of methods normally used in coronary arteries to restore Circulatory system to the lower extremities. Unlike angioplasty and stents of blocked arteries that simply push blockages aside into the wall of the artery, Atherectomy involved inserting a thin catheter with a scraping blade is inserted into the artery.

Chapter 1. PART I: Chapter 1 - Chapter 4

Cardiopulmonary bypass	Cardiopulmonary bypass (CPB) is a technique that temporarily takes over the function of the heart and lungs during surgery, maintaining the circulation of blood and the oxygen content of the body. The CPB pump itself is often referred to as a Heart-Lung Machine or the Pump. Cardiopulmonary bypass pumps are operated by allied health professionals known as perfusionists in association with surgeons who connect the pump to the patient's body.
Ciliary body	The Ciliary body is the circumferential tissue inside the eye composed of the ciliary muscle and ciliary processes. It is triangular in horizontal section, and is coated by a double layer, the ciliary epithelium. The inner layer is transparent and covers the vitreous body, and is continuous from the neural tissue of the retina.
Electrophysiology	Electrophysiology is the study of the electrical properties of biological cells and tissues. It involves measurements of voltage change or electric current on a wide variety of scales from single ion channel proteins to whole organs like the heart. In neuroscience, it includes measurements of the electrical activity of neurons, and particularly action potential activity.
Embolectomy	Embolectomy is the removal of a blockage in a blood vessel: the surgical removal of an embolus, usually a blood clot or other obstruction, in a blood vessel. Typically this is done by inserting a catheter with an inflatable balloon attached to its tip into an artery, passing the catheter tip beyond the clot, inflating the ballon, and removing the clot by withdrawing the catheter.
Endarterectomy	Endarterectomy is a surgical procedure to remove the atheromatous plaque material, or blockage, in the lining of an artery constricted by the buildup of soft/hardening deposits. It is carried out by separating the plaque from the arterial wall. It was first performed on a superficial femoral artery in 1946 by the Portuguese surgeon João Cid dos Santos.
Epicardial	Epicardial is a term used by some cardiac surgeons meaning ` on the outside of the cardiac muscle`.
Fistula	In medicine, a Fistula (pl. Fistulas or Fistulae) is an abnormal connection or passageway between two epithelium-lined organs or vessels that normally do not connect. It is generally a disease condition, but a Fistula may be surgically created for therapeutic reasons.

Chapter 1. PART I: Chapter 1 - Chapter 4

Hemolysis	Hemolysis (or haemolysis)--from the Greek Hemo-, Greek Aá¼·μα meaning blood, -lysis, meaning to break open--is the breaking open of red blood cells and the release of hemoglobin into the surrounding fluid .
	In vivo (inside the body) Hemolysis, which can be caused by a large number of conditions, can lead to anemia.
	Anemias caused by in vivo Hemolysis are collectively called hemolytic anemias.
Nerve	A Nerve is an enclosed, cable-like bundle of peripheral axons (the long, slender projections of neurons). A Nerve provides a common pathway for the electrochemical Nerve impulses that are transmitted along each of the axons. Nerves are found only in the peripheral nervous system.
Pericardiocentesis	In medicine, Pericardiocentesis is a procedure where fluid is aspirated from the pericardium (the sac enveloping the heart).
	It is generally done under ultrasound guidance, to minimize complications. There are two locations that Pericardiocentesis can be performed without puncturing the lungs.
	· One location is through the 5th or 6th intercostal space at the left sternal border at the cardiac notch of the left lung.
	· The other location is through the infrasternal angle.
Cardiology	Cardiology is a specialty dealing with disorders of the heart and blood vessels. The field includes diagnosis and treatment of congenital heart defects, coronary artery disease, heart failure, valvular heart disease and electrophysiology. Physicians specializing in this field of medicine are called cardiologists.
Diabetes	Diabetes mellitus --often referred to as diabetes--is a condition in which the body either does not produce enough, or does not properly respond to, insulin, a hormone produced in the pancreas. Insulin enables cells to absorb glucose in order to turn it into energy. This causes glucose to accumulate in the blood , leading to various potential complications.

	Many types of diabetes are recognized: The principal three are: · Type 1: Results from the body`s failure to produce insulin.
Coronary artery disease	Coronary artery disease is the end result of the accumulation of atheromatous plaques within the walls of the coronary arteries that supply the myocardium (the muscle of the heart) with oxygen and nutrients. It is sometimes also called coronary heart disease (CHD), but although Coronary artery disease is the most common cause of CHD, it is not the only cause. Coronary artery disease is the leading cause of death worldwide.
Ischemia	In medicine, Ischemia is a restriction in blood supply, generally due to factors in the blood vessels, with resultant damage or dysfunction of tissue. It may also be spelled ischaemia or ischæmia. Rather than hypoxia , Ischemia is an absolute or relative shortage of the blood supply to an organ, i.e. a shortage of oxygen, glucose and other blood-borne fuels.
Vascular	Vascular in zoology and medicine means `related to blood vessels`, which are part of the circulatory system. An organ or tissue that is Vascularized is heavily endowed with blood vessels and thus richly supplied with blood. In botany, plants with a dedicated transport system for water and nutrients are called Vascular plants.
Procedures	An ASC is a health care facility that specializes in providing surgery, including certain pain management and diagnostic (e.g., colonoscopy) services in an outpatient setting. Overall, the services provided can be generally called procedures. In simple terms, ASC-qualified procedures can be considered procedures that are more intensive than those done in the average doctor`s office but not so intensive as to require a hospital stay.

Chapter 1. PART I: Chapter 1 - Chapter 4

Blood pressure	Blood pressure is the pressure (force per unit area) exerted by circulating blood on the walls of blood vessels, and constitutes one of the principal vital signs. The pressure of the circulating blood decreases as it moves away from the heart through arteries and capillaries, and toward the heart through veins. When unqualified, the term Blood pressure usually refers to brachial arterial pressure: that is, in the major blood vessel of the upper left or right arm that takes blood away from the heart.
Essential hypertension	Essential hypertension is the form of hypertension that by definition, has no identifiable cause. It is the most common type of hypertension, affecting 95% of hypertensive patients, it tends to be familial and is likely to be the consequence of an interaction between environmental and genetic factors. Prevalence of Essential hypertension increases with age, and individuals with relatively high blood pressures at younger ages are at increased risk for the subsequent development of hypertension.
Hypertension	Hypertension is a chronic medical condition in which the blood pressure is elevated. It is also referred to as high blood pressure or shortened to HT, HTN or HPN. The word `Hypertension`, by itself, normally refers to systemic, arterial Hypertension. Hypertension can be classified as either essential (primary) or secondary.
Hypotension	In physiology and medicine, Hypotension refers to an abnormally low blood pressure. This is best understood as a physiologic state, rather than a disease. It is often associated with shock, though not necessarily indicative of it.
Orthostatic hypotension	Orthostatic hypotension (also known as postural hypotension, and, colloquially, as head rush or a dizzy spell and to some people `the elevator effect`) is a form of hypotension in which a person's blood pressure suddenly falls when the person stands up. The decrease is typically greater than 20/10 mm Hg, and may be most pronounced after resting. The incidence increases with age.
Pseudoaneurysm	A Pseudoaneurysm, also known as a false aneurysm, is a hematoma that forms as the result of a leaking hole in an artery. Note that the hematoma forms outside the arterial wall, so it is contained by the surrounding tissues. Also it must continue to communicate with the artery to be considered a Pseudoaneurysm.
Thrombus	A Thrombus , or blood clot, is the final product of the blood coagulation step in hemostasis. It is achieved via the aggregation of platelets that form a platelet plug, and the activation of the humoral coagulation system . A Thrombus is normal in cases of injury, but pathologic in instances of thrombosis.

Clam\101

Chapter 1. PART I: Chapter 1 - Chapter 4

Phlebitis	Phlebitis is an inflammation of a vein, usually in the legs. When Phlebitis is associated with the formation of blood clots (thrombosis), usually in the deep veins of the legs, the condition is called thromboPhlebitis. These clots can travel to the lungs, causing pulmonary embolisms which can be fatal.
Thrombophlebitis	Thrombophlebitis is phlebitis (vein inflammation) related to a blood clot or thrombus. When it occurs repeatedly in different locations, it is known as `Thrombophlebitis migrans` or `migrating Thrombophlebitis`. Thrombophlebitis (another medical term is `White Leg`) is related to a blood clot (thrombus) in the vein.
Varicose veins	Varicose veins are veins that have become enlarged and tortuous. The term commonly refers to the veins on the leg,although varicose veins can occur elsewhere. Veins have leaflet valves to prevent blood from flowing backwards (retrograde).
Heart failure	Heart failure is a condition in which a problem with the structure or function of the heart impairs its ability to supply sufficient blood flow to meet the body`s needs. It should not be confused with cardiac arrest . Common causes of Heart failure include myocardial infarction and other forms of ischemic heart disease, hypertension, valvular heart disease and cardiomyopathy.
Atrioventricular block	An Atrioventricular block involves the impairment of the conduction between the atria and ventricles of the heart. Strong vagal stimulation may produce AV block. The cholinergic receptor types affected are the muscarinic receptors. There are three types: · First degree AV block - PR interval greater than 0.20sec. · Second degree AV block - Type 1 (aka Mobitz 1, Wenkebach): Progressive prolongation of PR interval with dropped beats .
Bradycardia	Bradycardia , as applied to adult medicine, is defined as a resting heart rate of under 60 beats per minute, though it is seldom symptomatic until the rate drops below 50 beat/min. Trained athletes or young healthy individuals may also have a slow resting heart rate . Resting Bradycardia is often considered normal if the individual has no other symptoms such as fatigue, weakness, dizziness, lightheadedness, fainting, chest discomfort, palpitations or shortness of breath associated with it.

Chapter 1. PART I: Chapter 1 - Chapter 4

Fibrillation	Fibrillation is the rapid, irregular, and unsynchronized contraction of muscle fibers. An important occurrence is with the heart. There are two major classes of cardiac Fibrillation: atrial Fibrillation and ventricular Fibrillation.
Infective endocarditis	Infective endocarditis is a form of endocarditis caused by infectious agents. The agents are usually bacterial, but other organisms can also be responsible. The valves of the heart do not receive any dedicated blood supply.
Ventricular fibrillation	Ventricular fibrillation is a condition in which there is uncoordinated contraction of the cardiac muscle of the ventricles in the heart, making them quiver rather than contract properly. While there is activity, perhaps best described as `writhing like a can filled with worms` it is undetectable by palpation (feeling) at major pulse points of the carotid and femoral arteries especially by the lay person. Such an arrhythmia is only confirmed by ECG/EKG. Ventricular fibrillation is a medical emergency that requires prompt BLS/ACLS interventions because should the arrhythmia continue for more than a few seconds, it will likely degenerate further into asystole (a flat ECG with no rhythm- which is usually not responsive to therapy unless there is still some residual fine Ventricular fibrillation rhythm left or the patient is otherwise lucky AND is treated very quickly); after this, within minutes blood circulation will cease, and sudden cardiac death (SCD) may occur in a matter of minutes and/or the patient could sustain irreversible brain damage and possibly be left brain dead (death often occurs if normal sinus rhythm is not restored within 90 seconds of the onset of Ventricular fibrillation, especially if it has degenerated further into asystole).
Endocarditis	Endocarditis is an inflammation of the inner layer of the heart, the endocardium. It usually involves the heart valves (native or prosthetic valves). Other structures which may be involved include the interventricular septum, the chordae tendinae, the mural endocardium, or even on intracardiac devices.
Rhythm	Rhythm is the variation of the length and accentuation of a series of sounds or other events. The study of Rhythm, stress, and pitch in speech is called prosody; it is a topic in linguistics. Narmour (1980, p. 147-53) describes three categories of prosodic rules which create Rhythmic successions which are additive (same duration repeated), cumulative (short-long), or countercumulative (long-short).
Pericarditis	Pericarditis is an inflammation (-itis) of the pericardium (the fibrous sac surrounding the heart).

Pericarditis can be classified according to the composition of the inflammatory exudate.

Types include:

· serous

· purulent

· fibrinous

· caseous

· hemorrhagic

· Post infarction
Pericardiocentesis can be performed to permit analysis of the pericardial fluid.

Acute Pericarditis is more common than chronic Pericarditis, and can occur as a complication of infections, immunologic conditions, or heart attack.

Rheumatic fever	Rheumatic fever is an inflammatory disease that may develop two to three weeks after a Group A streptococcal infection (such as strep throat or scarlet fever). It is believed to be caused by antibody cross-reactivity and can involve the heart, joints, skin, and brain. Acute Rheumatic fever commonly appears in children between ages 5 and 15, with only 20% of first time attacks occurring in adults.
Fever	Fever is a frequent medical sign that describes an increase in internal body temperature to levels above normal. Fever is most accurately characterized as a temporary elevation in the body's thermoregulatory set-point, usually by about 1-2 °C . Fever is caused by an elevation in the thermoregulatory set-point, causing typical body temperature (generally and problematically considered to be 37 °C or 98.6 °F) to rise, and effector mechanisms are enacted as a result.
Stenosis	A Stenosis is an abnormal narrowing in a blood vessel or other tubular organ or structure.

	It is also sometimes called a `stricture` . The term `coarctation` is synonymous, but is commonly used only in the context of aortic coarctation.
Acute pericarditis	Acute pericarditis is an inflammation of the sac surrounding the heart --- the pericardium --- usually lasting < 6 weeks. It is by far the most common condition affecting the pericardium. According to a recent article, the most common causes of Acute pericarditis include: · (35%) Neoplastic · (23%) Autoimmune · (21%) Viral - adenovirus, enterovirus, cytomegalovirus, influenza virus, hepatitis B virus, and herpes simplex virus, etc · (6%) Bacterial (other than tuberculosis) · (6%) Uremia · (4%) Tuberculosis · (4%) Idiopathic · (remaining) trauma, drugs, post-AMI, myocarditis, dissecting aortic aneurysm, radiation Chest pain is one of the common symptoms of Acute pericarditis.
Aortic valve	The aortic valve is one of the valves of the heart. It is normally tricuspid (with three leaflets), although in 1% of the population it is found to be congenitally bicuspid (two leaflets). It lies between the left ventricle and the aorta.
Aortic valve stenosis	Aortic valve stenosis is a valvular heart disease caused by the incomplete opening of the aortic valve.

Chapter 1. PART I: Chapter 1 - Chapter 4

	The aortic valve controls the direction of blood flow from the left ventricle to the aorta. When in good working order, the aortic valve does not impede the flow of blood between these two spaces.
Mitral regurgitation	Mitral regurgitation, mitral insufficiency or mitral incompetence is a disorder of the heart in which the mitral valve does not close properly when the heart pumps out blood. It is the abnormal leaking of blood from the left ventricle, through the mitral valve, and into the left atrium, when the left ventricle contracts, i.e. there is regurgitation of blood back into the left atrium. Mitral regurgitation is the most common form of valvular heart disease.
Mitral valve	The Mitral valve is a dual-flap valve in the heart that lies between the left atrium and the left ventricle (LV). The Mitral valve and the tricuspid valve are known collectively as the atrioventricular valves because they lie between the atria and the ventricles of the heart and control the flow of blood.

A normally-functioning Mitral valve opens secondary to increased pressure from the left atrium as it fills with blood. |
| Pulmonic regurgitation | Pulmonic regurgitation, also known as pulmonary regurgitation, is the backward flow of blood from the pulmonary artery, through the pulmonary valve, and into the right ventricle of the heart during diastole. While a small amount of Pulmonic regurgitation may occur in healthy individuals, it is usually detectable only by an echocardiogram and is harmless. More pronounced regurgitation that is noticed through a routine physical examination is a medical sign of disease and warrants further investigation. |
| Cardiomyopathy | Cardiomyopathy, which literally means `heart muscle disease,` is the deterioration of the function of the myocardium (i.e., the actual heart muscle) for any reason. People with Cardiomyopathy are often at risk of arrhythmia or sudden cardiac death or both.

Cardiomyopathies can generally be categorized into two groups, based on World Health Organization guidelines: extrinsic cardiomyopathies and intrinsic cardiomyopathies. |
| Coarctation | A stenosis is an abnormal narrowing in a blood vessel or other tubular organ or structure.

It is also sometimes called a `stricture` .

The term `Coarctation` is synonymous, but is commonly used only in the context of aortic Coarctation. |

Chapter 1. PART I: Chapter 1 - Chapter 4

Congenital heart defect	A Congenital heart defect is a defect in the structure of the heart and great vessels of a newborn. Most heart defects either obstruct blood flow in the heart or vessels near it or cause blood to flow through the heart in an abnormal pattern, although other defects affecting heart rhythm (such as long QT syndrome) can also occur. Heart defects are among the most common birth defects and are the leading cause of birth defect-related deaths.
Constrictive pericarditis	In many cases, Constrictive pericarditis is a late sequela of an inflammatory condition of the pericardium. The inflammatory condition is usually an infection that involves the pericardium, but it may be after a heart attack or after heart surgery. Almost half the cases of Constrictive pericarditis in the developing world are idiopathic in origin.
Dilated cardiomyopathy	Dilated cardiomyopathy or DCM is a condition in which the heart becomes weakened and enlarged, and cannot pump blood efficiently. The decreased heart function can affect the lungs, liver, and other body systems. DCM is one of the cardiomyopathies, a group of diseases that primarily affect the myocardium (the muscle of the heart).
Hypertrophic cardiomyopathy	Hypertrophic cardiomyopathy is the leading cause of sudden cardiac death (SCD) in young athletes. Hypertrophic cardiomyopathyM is a genetic disorder that causes the muscle of the heart (the myocardium) to thicken (or hypertrophy) without any apparent reason. When the heart thickens and becomes enlarged, particularly at the septum and left ventricle, it can cause dangerous arrhythmias (abnormal heart rhythms).
Patella	The Patella is a thick, circular-triangular bone which articulates with the femur and covers and protects the knee joint. It is the largest sesamoid bone in the human body. It is attached to the tendon of the quadriceps femoris muscle, which contracts to extend/straighten the knee.
Pericardial effusion	Pericardial effusion is an abnormal accumulation of fluid in the pericardial cavity. Because of the limited amount of space in the pericardial cavity, fluid accumulation will lead to an increased intrapericardial pressure and this can negatively affect heart function. When there is a Pericardial effusion with enough pressure to adversely affect heart function, this is called cardiac tamponade.
Restrictive cardiomyopathy	Restrictive cardiomyopathy is a form of cardiomyopathy in which the walls are rigid, and the heart is restricted from stretching and filling with blood properly.

Chapter 1. PART I: Chapter 1 - Chapter 4

	It is the least common cardiomyopathy.
	Rhythmicity and contractility of the heart may be normal, but the stiff walls of the heart chambers (atria and ventricles) keep them from adequately filling, reducing preload and end-diastolic volume.
Effusion	In chemistry, Effusion is the process in which individual molecules flow through a hole without collisions between molecules. This occurs if the diameter of the hole is considerably smaller than the mean free path of the molecules. According to Graham`s law, the rate at which gases effuse (i.e., how many molecules pass through the hole per second) is dependent on their molecular weight; gases with a lower molecular weight effuse more quickly than gases with a higher molecular weight.
Tetralogy of Fallot	Tetralogy of Fallot is a congenital heart defect which is classically understood to involve four anatomical abnormalities (although only three of them are always present). It is the most common cyanotic heart defect, representing 55-70%, and the most common cause of blue baby syndrome.
	It was described in 1672 by Niels Stensen, in 1773 by Edward Sandifort, and in 1888 by the French physician Étienne-Louis Arthur Fallot, for whom it is named.

Clitoris	The Clitoris is a sexual organ that is present only in female mammals. In humans, the visible button-like portion is located near the anterior junction of the labia minora, above the opening of the urethra and vagina. Unlike the penis, which is homologous to the Clitoris, the Clitoris does not contain the distal portion of the urethra.
Fallopian tube	The Fallopian tubes also known as oviducts, uterine tubes, and salpinges (singular salpinx) are two very fine tubes lined with ciliated epithelia, leading from the ovaries of female mammals into the uterus, via the utero-tubal junction.
	The tube connects the ovary to something else as the egg passes through it in a woman`s body.
	The Fallopian tubes are a path in which an egg will travel through in order to reach the male sperm which was released from the male.
Labia majora	The Labia majora` (singular: labium majus) are two prominent longitudinal cutaneous folds which extend downward and backward from the mons pubis to the perineum and form the lateral boundaries of the cleft of venus, which contains the labia minora, interlabial sulci, clitoral hood, clitoral glans, frenulum clitoridis, the Hart`s Line, and the vulval vestibule, which contains the external openings of the urethra and the vagina.
	Each labium majus has two surfaces, an outer, pigmented and covered with strong, crisp hairs; and an inner, smooth and beset with large sebaceous follicles.
	Between the two there is a considerable quantity of areolar tissue, fat, and a tissue resembling the dartos tunic of the scrotum, besides vessels, nerves, and glands.
Labia minora	The Labia minora or nymphae are two longitudinal cutaneous folds on the human vulva. They are situated between the labia majora, and extend from the clitoris obliquely downward, laterally, and backward on either side of the vulval vestibule, ending between bottom of the vulval vestibule and the labia majora. In the virgin the posterior ends of the Labia minora are usually joined across the middle line by a fold of skin, named the frenulum labiorum pudendi or fourchette.

Chapter 2. PART II: Chapter 5 - Chapter 8

Ovaries	The ovary is an ovum-producing reproductive organ, often found in pairs as part of the vertebrate female reproductive system. ovaries in females are homologous to testes in males, in that they are both gonads and endocrine glands.
	ovaries are oval shaped and, in the human, measure approximately 3 cm x 1.5 cm x 1.5 cm .
Urinary meatus	The Urinary meatus is the external orifice of the urethra, from which urine is ejected during urination and semen is ejected during ejaculation.
	· Meatal stenosis .
Uterus	The Uterus is a major female hormone-responsive reproductive sex organ of most mammals, including humans. It is within the Uterus that the fetus develops during gestation. The term Uterus is used consistently within the medical and related professions; the Germanic term, womb is more common in everyday usage.
Vagina	The Vagina is a fibromuscular tubular tract leading from the uterus to the exterior of the body in female placental mammals and marsupials, or to the cloaca in female birds, monotremes, and some reptiles. Female insects and other invertebrates also have a Vagina, which is the terminal part of the oviduct. The Latinate plural is Vaginae.
Vomer	The Vomer is one of the unpaired facial bones of the skull. It is located in the midsagittal line, and articulates with the sphenoid, the ethmoid, the left and right palatine bones, and the left and right maxillary bones.
	The Vomeronasal organ, also called Jacobson's organ, is a chemoreceptor organ named for its closeness to the Vomer and nasal bones, and is particularly developed in animals such as cats , and is thought to have to do with the perception of certain pheromones.
Gland	A gland is an organ in an animal's body that synthesizes a substance for release such as hormones or breast milk, often into the bloodstream (endocrine gland) or into cavities inside the body or its outer surface (exocrine gland).

glands can be divided into 3 groups:

· Endocrine glands -- are glands that secrete their products through the basal lamina and lack a duct system.

· Exocrine glands -- secrete their products through a duct or directly onto the apical surface, the glands in this group can be divided into three groups:

· Apocrine glands -- a portion of the secreting cell`s body is lost during secretion. Apocrine gland is often used to refer to the apocrine sweat glands, however it is thought that apocrine sweat glands may not be true apocrine glands as they may not use the apocrine method of secretion.

· Holocrine glands -- the entire cell disintegrates to secrete its substances (e.g., sebaceous glands)

· Merocrine glands -- cells secrete their substances by exocytosis (e.g., mucous and serous glands). Also called `eccrine.`
The type of secretory product of an Exocrine gland may also be one of three categories:

· Serous glands -- secrete a watery, often protein-rich product.

· Mucous glands -- secrete a viscous product, rich in carbohydrates (e.g., glycoproteins).

· Sebaceous glands -- secrete a lipid product.
the third type; mixed

Every gland is formed by an ingrowth from an epithelial surface.

Menstruation	Menstruation is the shedding of the uterine lining (endometrium). It occurs on a regular basis in reproductive-age females of certain mammal species. Overt Menstruation is found primarily in humans and close evolutionary relatives such as chimpanzees.

Pregnancy	Pregnancy is the carrying of one or more offspring, known as a fetus or embryo, inside the uterus of a female. In a pregnancy, there can be multiple gestations, as in the case of twins or triplets. Human pregnancy is the most studied of all mammalian pregnancies.
Abortion	An Abortion is the termination of a pregnancy by the removal or expulsion from the uterus of a fetus/embryo, resulting in or caused by its death. An Abortion can occur spontaneously due to complications during pregnancy or can be induced, in humans and other species. In the context of human pregnancies, an Abortion induced to preserve the health of the gravida (pregnant female) is termed a therapeutic Abortion, while an Abortion induced for any other reason is termed an elective Abortion.
Amniocentesis	Amniocentesis (also referred to as amniotic fluid test or AFT), is a medical procedure used in prenatal diagnosis of chromosomal abnormalities and fetal infections , in which a small amount of amniotic fluid, which contains fetal tissues, is extracted from the amnion or amniotic sac surrounding a developing fetus, and the fetal DNA is examined for genetic abnormalities. Before the start of the procedure, a local anesthetic can be given to the mother in order to relieve the pain felt during the insertion of the needle used to withdraw the fluid. After the local is in effect, a needle is usually inserted through the mother's abdominal wall, then through the wall of the uterus, and finally into the amniotic sac.
Amniotic sac	The Amniotic sac is the sac in which the fetus develops in amniotes. Its wall is the amnion, the inner of the two fetal membranes. It encloses the amniotic cavity and the embryo.
Cervical	In anatomy, `Cervical` is an adjective that has two meanings: · of or pertaining to any neck. · of or pertaining to the female cervix: i.e., the neck of the uterus. · Commonly used medical phrases involving the neck are · Cervical collar · Cervical disc (intervertebral disc)

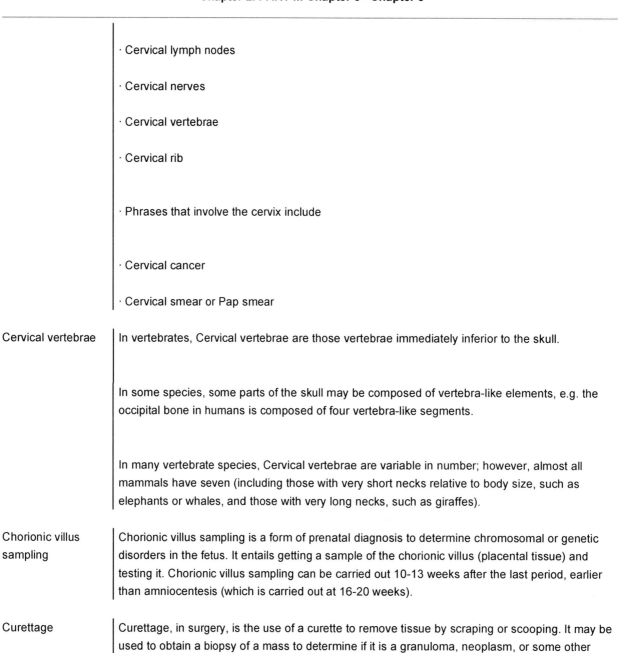

· Cervical lymph nodes

· Cervical nerves

· Cervical vertebrae

· Cervical rib

· Phrases that involve the cervix include

· Cervical cancer

· Cervical smear or Pap smear

Cervical vertebrae	In vertebrates, Cervical vertebrae are those vertebrae immediately inferior to the skull. In some species, some parts of the skull may be composed of vertebra-like elements, e.g. the occipital bone in humans is composed of four vertebra-like segments. In many vertebrate species, Cervical vertebrae are variable in number; however, almost all mammals have seven (including those with very short necks relative to body size, such as elephants or whales, and those with very long necks, such as giraffes).
Chorionic villus sampling	Chorionic villus sampling is a form of prenatal diagnosis to determine chromosomal or genetic disorders in the fetus. It entails getting a sample of the chorionic villus (placental tissue) and testing it. Chorionic villus sampling can be carried out 10-13 weeks after the last period, earlier than amniocentesis (which is carried out at 16-20 weeks).
Curettage	Curettage, in surgery, is the use of a curette to remove tissue by scraping or scooping. It may be used to obtain a biopsy of a mass to determine if it is a granuloma, neoplasm, or some other tumor. It is often employed prior to definitive excisional surgery to more precisely delineate the extent of a tumor.

Cystocele	A Cystocele is a medical condition that occurs when the tough fibrous wall between a woman's bladder and her vagina is torn by childbirth, allowing the bladder to herniate into the vagina. Urethroceles often occur with Cystoceles. This condition may cause discomfort and problems with emptying the bladder.
Dilation	Dilation refers to an enlargement or expansion in bulk or extent, the opposite of contraction. It derives from the Latin dilatare, 'to spread wide'. In physiology: · Pupillary response, Dilation of the pupil of the eye · Cervical Dilation, the widening of the cervix in childbirth, miscarriage etc. · Dilation and curettage, the opening of the cervix and surgical removal of the contents of the uterus · VasoDilation, the widening of luminal diameter in blood vessels In mathematics: · Dilation, a function from a metric space into itself · Dilation , a Dilation of an operator on a Hilbert space · Dilation an operation in mathematical morphology · Homothety, the scalar multiplication operator on a vector space In physics:

· Scale invariance, a feature of objects or laws that do not change if length scales (or energy scales) are multiplied by a common factor

· Time Dilation, the observation that another`s clock is ticking at a slower rate as measured by one`s own clock
In music:

· Dilate (Bardo Pond album)

· Dilate (Ani DiFranco album)

Ectopic

In medicine an ectopia is a displacement or malposition of an organ of the body. Most ectopias are congenital but some may happen later in life.

· Ectopia lentis is the displacement of the crystalline lens of the eye

· Ectopia cordis is the displacement of the heart outside the body during fetal development

· Renal ectopia occurs when both kidneys occur on the same side of the body

· ectopic pregnancy occurs when the fertilized egg implants anywhere other than the uterine wall

· Cardiac ectopy occurs when electrical signals for a heartbeat originate in the wrong part of the heart muscle.
In molecular biology the term ectopic is used for at least three purposes:

· ectopic recombination refers to recombination between sites, usually containing identical or similar sequences, at different locations in the genome, leading to deletions, insertions, or chromosomal crossovers

· a gene is ectopically expressed when it is expressed in an abnormal place.

· in transgenic experiments, ectopic integration indicates the insertion of the transgene at a site other than its natural chromosomal locus

Hysterectomy	A Hysterectomy is the surgical removal of the uterus, usually performed by a gynecologist. Hysterectomy may be total ` href=`/wiki/Fundus_(uterus)`>fundus, and cervix of the uterus; often called `complete`) or partial (removal of the uterine body but leaving the cervical stump, also called `supracervical`). It is the most commonly performed gynecological surgical procedure.
Hysteroscopy	Hysteroscopy is the inspection of the uterine cavity by endoscopy. It allows for the diagnosis of intrauterine pathology and serves as a method for surgical intervention (operative Hysteroscopy). The hysteroscope is an optical instrument connected to a video unit with a fiber optic light source, and to the channels for delivery and removal of a distention medium.
Leukemia	Leukemia is a cancer of the blood or bone marrow and is characterized by an abnormal proliferation (production by multiplication) of blood cells, usually white blood cells (leukocytes). Leukemia is a broad term covering a spectrum of diseases. In turn, it is part of the even broader group of diseases called hematological neoplasms.
Nervous system	The Nervous system is an organ system containing a network of specialized cells called neurons that coordinate the actions of an animal and transmit signals between different parts of its body. In most animals the Nervous system consists of two parts, central and peripheral. The central Nervous system contains the brain and spinal cord.
Introitus	The Introitus is an entrance that goes into a canal or hollow organ. Introitus is another name for the vaginal orifice.

Introitus has also been used for classifying uterine prolapse:

· 1st degree prolapse: cervix is in the vagina

· 2nd degree: cervix at the level of the Introitus

· 3rd degree: cervix comes out of the Introitus

· procidentia: the uterus also comes out of the Introitus .

Chapter 2. PART II: Chapter 5 - Chapter 8

Mitral regurgitation	Mitral regurgitation, mitral insufficiency or mitral incompetence is a disorder of the heart in which the mitral valve does not close properly when the heart pumps out blood. It is the abnormal leaking of blood from the left ventricle, through the mitral valve, and into the left atrium, when the left ventricle contracts, i.e. there is regurgitation of blood back into the left atrium. Mitral regurgitation is the most common form of valvular heart disease.
Multiple sclerosis	Multiple sclerosis is a disease in which the fatty myelin sheaths around the axons of the brain and spinal cord are damaged, leading to demyelination and scarring as well as a broad spectrum of signs and symptoms. Disease onset usually occurs in young adults, and it is more common in females. It has a prevalence that ranges between 2 and 150 per 100,000. Multiple sclerosis was first described in 1868 by Jean-Martin Charcot.
Oophorectomy	Oophorectomy is the surgical removal of an ovary or ovaries. In the case of non-human animals, it is also called spaying and is a form of sterilization. Removal of the ovaries in women is the biological equivalent of castration in males, and the term is occasionally used in the medical literature instead of Oophorectomy.
Placenta	The Placenta is an organ that connects the developing fetus to the uterine wall to allow nutrient uptake, waste elimination and gas exchange via the mother's blood supply. Placentas are a defining characteristic of eutherian or `Placental` mammals, but are also found in some snakes and lizards with varying levels of development up to mammalian levels. The word Placenta comes from the Latin for cake, from Greek plakóenta/plakoúnta, accusative of plakóeis/plakoús - πλακΐŒεις, πλακοΪ ς, `flat, slab-like`, in reference to its round, flat appearance in humans.
Salpingectomy	Salpingectomy refers to the surgical removal of a Fallopian tube. The procedure was first performed by Lawson Tait in patients with a bleeding ectopic pregnancy; this procedure has since saved the lives of countless women. Other indications for a Salpingectomy include infected tubes, (as in a hydrosalpinx) or as part of the surgical procedure for tubal cancer.
Tumor	A tumor or tumour is the name for a swelling or lesion formed by an abnormal growth of cells (termed neoplastic). tumor is not synonymous with cancer. A tumor can be benign, pre-malignant or malignant, whereas cancer is by definition malignant.
Disease	A Disease or medical condition is an abnormal condition of an organism that impairs bodily functions, associated with specific symptoms and signs. It may be caused by external factors, such as invading organisms, or it may be caused by internal dysfunctions, such as autoimmune Diseases.

	In human beings, `Disease` is often used more broadly to refer to any condition that causes pain, dysfunction, distress, social problems, and/or death to the person afflicted, or similar problems for those in contact with the person.
Fistula	In medicine, a Fistula (pl. Fistulas or Fistulae) is an abnormal connection or passageway between two epithelium-lined organs or vessels that normally do not connect. It is generally a disease condition, but a Fistula may be surgically created for therapeutic reasons.
Hormone	A Hormone is a chemical released by one or more cells that affects cells in other parts of the organism. Only a small amount of Hormone is required to alter cell metabolism. It is essentially a chemical messenger that transports a signal from one cell to another.
Kidney	The Kidneys are paired organs, which have the production of urine as their primary function. Kidneys are seen in many types of animals, including vertebrates and some invertebrates. They are an essential part of the urinary system, but have several secondary functions concerned with homeostatic functions.
Metastasis	Metastasis , or metastatic disease, sometimes abbreviated mets, is the spread of a disease from one organ or part to another non-adjacent organ or part. It had been previously thought that only malignant tumor cells and infections have the capacity to metastasize; however, this is being reconsidered due to new research. Cancer cells can break away, leak, or spill from a primary tumor, enter lymphatic and blood vessels, circulate through the bloodstream, and be deposited within normal tissue elsewhere in the body.
Regurgitation	Regurgitation, Regurgiate or Regurgitate can refer to: · Regurgitation · Vomiting · Regurgitation · Regurgitate (band), a goregrind band `

Chapter 2. PART II: Chapter 5 - Chapter 8

Sclerosis	Sclerosis or sclerotization is a hardening of tissue and other anatomical features; · Sclerosis · Cyberbrain Sclerosis, a fictional disease introduced in Ghost in the Shell: Stand Alone Complex. The disease is characterized by hardening of the brain tissues precipitated by the cyberization process. · a process which hardens plant tissue by adding fibers and sclereids, resulting in sclerenchyma
Amenorrhea	Amenorrhoea (BE), Amenorrhea or amenorrhÅ"a, is the absence of a menstrual period in a woman of reproductive age. Physiological states of amenorrhoea are seen during pregnancy and lactation (breastfeeding), the latter also forming the basis of a form of contraception known as the lactational Amenorrhea method. Outside of the reproductive years there is absence of menses during childhood and after menopause.
Dysmenorrhea	Dysmenorrhea is a medical condition characterized by severe uterine pain during menstruation. While most women experience minor pain during menstruation, Dysmenorrhea is diagnosed when the pain is so severe as to limit normal activities, or require medication. Dysmenorrhea can feature different kinds of pain, including sharp, throbbing, dull, nauseating, burning, or shooting pain.
Dysfunctional uterine bleeding	Dysfunctional uterine bleeding is abnormal genital tract bleeding based in the uterus and found in the absence of demonstrable organic pathology, and is the most common cause of functional abnormal uterine bleeding. Diagnosis must be made by exclusion, since organic pathology must first be ruled out. It can be classified as ovulatory or anovulatory, depending on whether ovulation is occurring or not.
Endometriosis	Endometriosis is a medical condition in women in which endometrial cells are deposited in areas outside the uterine cavity. The uterine cavity is lined by endometrial cells, which are under the influence of female hormones. Endometrial cells deposited in areas outside the uterus (Endometriosis) continue to be influenced by these hormonal changes and respond similarly as do those cells found inside the uterus.

Hypomenorrhea	Hypomenorrhea scanty periods, and spotting at periods, is extremely light menstrual blood flow. It is the opposite of Hypermenorrhea which is more properly called Menorrhagia. One cause of Hypomenorrhea is Asherman`s syndrome (intrauterine adhesions), of which Hypomenorrhea may be the only apparent sign.
Menometrorrhagia	Menometrorrhagia is a condition in which prolonged or excessive uterine bleeding occurs irregularly and more frequently than normal. It can occur due to any of several causes, including hormonal imbalance, endometriosis, uterine fibroids, or cancer. It can lead to anemia in long-standing cases.....
Menorrhagia	Menorrhagia is an abnormally heavy and prolonged menstrual period at regular intervals. Causes may be due to abnormal blood clotting, disruption of normal hormonal regulation of periods or disorders of the endometrial lining of the uterus. Depending upon the cause, it may be associated with abnormally painful periods (dysmenorrhea).
Mental foramen	The Mental foramen is one of two holes (`foramina`) located on the anterior surface of the mandible. It permits passage of the mental nerve and vessels. The Mental foramen descends slightly in edentulous individuals.
Metrorrhagia	Metrorrhagia refers to vaginal bleeding among premenopausal women that is not synchronized with their menstrual period. It is often referred to as spotting. Uterine bleeding at irregular intervals, particularly between the expected menstrual periods, may or may not be associate with the post-menopausal period. · endometriosis · adenomyosis · ectopic pregnancy · hormone imbalance · endometrial hyperplasia

· polyp

· Ketosis Diets

· Use of progestin-only contraceptives, such as Depo Provera

· use of an IUD

· cervical cancer

· Uterine leiomyomas

· Enlarged uterus with dysmennorrhea

· Occasionally ovulation

· Pregnancy (implantation bleeding)

· sexually Transmitted Disease

· Von Willebrand Disease

· [Pelvic Inflammatory Disease]

Oligomenorrhea	Oligomenorrhea is the medical term for infrequent uterine bleeding episodes with intervals of more than 35 days. The duration of such events may vary.

Oligomenorrhea can also be a result of prolactinomas (adenomas of the anterior pituitary). |
| Premenstrual syndrome | Premenstrual syndrome (PMS) is a collection of physical, psychological, and emotional symptoms related to a woman`s menstrual cycle. While most women (about 80 percent) of child-bearing age have some symptoms of PMS, the official definition limits the scope to having symptoms of `sufficient severity to interfere with some aspects of life`. Such symptoms are usually predictable and occur regularly during the two weeks prior to menses. |
| Foramen | In anatomy, a Foramen is any opening. Many foramina transmit muscle or a nerve. |

	.
Syndrome	In medicine and psychology, the term syndrome refers to the association of several clinically recognizable features, signs (observed by a physician), symptoms (reported by the patient), phenomena or characteristics that often occur together, so that the presence of one feature alerts the physician to the presence of the others. In recent decades the term has been used outside of medicine to refer to a combination of phenomena seen in association. The term syndrome derives from its Greek roots and means literally `run together`, as the features do.
Candidiasis	Candidiasis or thrush is a fungal infection (mycosis) of any of the Candida species, of which Candida albicans is the most common. Candidiasis encompasses infections that range from superficial, such as oral thrush and vaginitis, to systemic and potentially life-threatening diseases. Candida infections of the latter category are also referred to as candidemia and are usually confined to severely immunocompromised persons, such as cancer, transplant, and AIDS patients.
Genital herpes	Herpes genitalis refers to a genital infection by herpes simplex virus. Following the classification HSV into two distinct categories of HSV-1 and HSV-2 in the 1960s, it was established that `HSV-2 was below the waist, HSV-1 was above the waist`. Although genital herpes is largely believed to be caused by HSV-2, genital HSV-1 infections are increasing and now exceed 50% in certain populations, and that rule of thumb no longer applies.
Genital wart	Genital warts is a highly contagious sexually transmitted disease caused by some sub-types of human papillomavirus (HPV). It is spread through direct skin-to-skin contact during oral, genital, or anal sex with an infected partner. Warts are the most easily recognized symptom of genital HPV infection.
Gonorrhea	Gonorrhea is a common sexually transmitted infection caused by the bacterium Neisseria gonorrhoeae . In the US, its incidence is second only to chlamydia among bacterial STDs. In both men and women if gonorrhea is left untreated, it may spread throughout the body, affecting joints and even heart valves.
Syphilis	Syphilis is a sexually transmitted disease caused by the spirochetal bacterium Treponema pallidum subspecies pallidum. The route of transmission of syphilis is almost always through sexual contact, although there are examples of congenital syphilis via transmission from mother to child in utero.

	The signs and symptoms of syphilis are numerous; before the advent of serological testing, precise diagnosis was very difficult.
Wart	A Wart is generally a small, rough tumor, typically on hands and feet but often other locations, that can resemble a cauliflower or a solid blister. Warts are common, and are caused by a viral infection, specifically by the human papillomavirus (HPV) and are contagious when in contact with the skin of an infected person. It is also possible to get Warts from using towels or other objects used by an infected person.
Fibroid	A uterine Fibroid is a non-cancerous tumor that originates from the smooth muscle layer (myometrium) and the accompanying connective tissue of the uterus. Fibroids are the most common benign tumors in females and typically found during the middle and later reproductive years. While most Fibroids are asymptomatic, they can grow and cause heavy and painful menstruation, painful sexual intercourse, and urinary frequency and urgency.
Fibromas	Fibromas are benign tumors that are composed of fibrous or connective tissue. They can grow in all organs, arising from mesenchyme tissue. The term `fibroblastic` or `fibromatous` is used to describe tumors of the fibrous connective tissue.
Left ventricle	The Left ventricle is one of four chambers (two atria and two ventricles) in the human heart. It receives oxygenated blood from the left atrium via the mitral valve, and pumps it into the aorta via the aortic valve.
	The Left ventricle is longer and more conical in shape than the right, and on transverse section its concavity presents an oval or nearly circular outline.
Leiomyoma	A Leiomyoma is a benign smooth muscle neoplasm that is not premalignant. They can occur in any organ, but the most common forms occur in the uterus, small bowel and the esophagus.
	· Greek: Oral contraceptive pills can be used to decrease excessive menstrual bleeding and pain associated with uterine fibroids.
	Uterine Leiomyomas originate in the myometrium and are classified by location:

	· Submucosal - lie just beneath the endometrium.
	· Intramural - lie within the uterine wall.
	· Subserosal - lie at the serosal surface of the uterus or may bulge out from the myometrium and can become pedunculated. They are also the most common benign esophageal tumour, though this accounts for less than 1% of esophageal neoplasms.
Myocardium	Cardiac muscle is a type of involuntary striated muscle found in the walls of the heart, specifically the Myocardium. Cardiac muscle cells are known as cardiac myocytes (or cardiomyocytes). Cardiac muscle is one of three major types of muscle, the others being skeletal and smooth muscle.
Myoma	Myoma is a kind of mesenchymal tumor. They are of two types. · The leioMyoma occurs in the skin or gut but the common form is the uterine fibroid. · RhabdoMyomas are rare tumors of muscles, they occur in childhood and often become malignant. To remove the tumor from the body, a myomectomy or hysterectomy is often required.
Trichomoniasis	Trichomoniasis, sometimes referred to as `trich`, is a common cause of vaginitis. It is a sexually transmitted disease. It is caused by the single-celled protozoan parasite Trichomonas vaginalis.
Uterine fibroid	A uterine fibroid is a non-cancerous tumor that originates from the smooth muscle layer (myometrium) and the accompanying connective tissue of the uterus. Fibroids are the most common benign tumors in females and typically found during the middle and later reproductive years. While most fibroids are asymptomatic, they can grow and cause heavy and painful menstruation, painful sexual intercourse, and urinary frequency and urgency.
Arteries	Arteries are blood vessels that carry blood away from the heart. All Arteries, with the exception of the pulmonary and umbilical Arteries, carry oxygenated blood.

	The circulatory system is extremely important for sustaining life.
Carotid arteries	In human anatomy, the common carotid artery is an artery that supplies the head and neck with oxygenated blood; it divides in the neck to form the external and internal Carotid arteries.
	The common carotid artery is a paired structure, meaning that there are two in the body, one for each half. The left and right common Carotid arteries follow the same course with the exception of their origin.
Fibroid	A uterine Fibroid is a non-cancerous tumor that originates from the smooth muscle layer (myometrium) and the accompanying connective tissue of the uterus. Fibroids are the most common benign tumors in females and typically found during the middle and later reproductive years. While most Fibroids are asymptomatic, they can grow and cause heavy and painful menstruation, painful sexual intercourse, and urinary frequency and urgency.
Adenocarcinoma	Adenocarcinoma is a cancer originating in glandular tissue. This tissue is also part of a larger tissue category known as epithelial. Epithelial tissue includes skin, glands and a variety of other tissue that lines the cavities and organs of the body.
Carcinoma	A Carcinoma is any malignant cancer that arises from epithelial cells. Carcinomas invade surrounding tissues and organs and may metastasize, or spread, to lymph nodes and other sites.
	Carcinoma in situ (CIS) is a pre-malignant condition, in which some cytological signs of malignancy are present, but there is no histological evidence of invasion through the epithelial basement membrane.
Invasive lobular carcinoma	Invasive lobular carcinoma is a type of breast cancer.
	Microscopically, it can present with a pattern known as `Indian filling`. The histology is also described as `single-file`.
Ductal carcinoma	Ductal carcinoma is a type of tumor that primarily presents in the ducts of a gland.
	Types include:

Chapter 2. PART II: Chapter 5 - Chapter 8

179

Go to **Cram101.com** for Interactive Practice Exams for this book or virtually any of your books.
And, **NEVER** highlight a book again!

	· Mammary Ductal carcinoma
	· Pancreatic Ductal carcinoma
Cervical cancer	Cervical cancer is malignant neoplasm of the cervix uteri or cervical area. It may present with vaginal bleeding but symptoms may be absent until the cancer is in its advanced stages. Treatment consists of surgery (including local excision) in early stages and chemotherapy and radiotherapy in advanced stages of the disease.
Endometrial cancer	Endometrial cancer refers to several types of malignancy which arise from the endometrium, or lining of the uterus. Endometrial cancers are the most common gynecologic cancers in the United States, with over 35,000 women diagnosed each year in the U.S. The most common subtype, endometrioid adenocarcinoma, typically occurs within a few decades of menopause, is associated with excessive estrogen exposure, often develops in the setting of endometrial hyperplasia, and presents most often with vaginal bleeding. Endometrial carcinoma is the third most common cause of gynecologic cancer death (behind ovarian and cervical cancer).
Cancer	Cancer is a genetic disorder in which the normal control of cell growth is lost. Cancer genetics is now one of the fastest expanding medical specialties. At the molecular level, Cancer is caused by mutation(s) in DNA, which result in aberrant cell proliferation.
Cervix	The Cervix is the lower, narrow portion of the uterus where it joins with the top end of the vagina. It is cylindrical or conical in shape and protrudes through the upper anterior vaginal wall. Approximately half its length is visible with appropriate medical equipment; the remainder lies above the vagina beyond view.
Germ cells	In biology, Germ cells are the cells that give rise to the gametes of organisms that reproduce sexually. In many animals, the Germ cells originate near the gut and migrate to the developing gonads. There, they undergo cell division of two types, mitosis and meiosis, followed by cellular differentiation into mature gametes, either eggs or sperm.
Reflux	Reflux is a technique involving the condensation of vapors and the return of this condensate to the system from which it originated. It is used in industrial and laboratory distillations. It is also used in chemistry to supply energy to reactions over a long period of time.
Tumor	A tumor or tumour is the name for a swelling or lesion formed by an abnormal growth of cells (termed neoplastic). tumor is not synonymous with cancer. A tumor can be benign, pre-malignant or malignant, whereas cancer is by definition malignant.

Chapter 2. PART II: Chapter 5 - Chapter 8

Facial muscles	The Facial muscles are a group of striated muscles innervated by the facial nerve that, among other things, control facial expression. These muscles are also called mimetic muscles. The Facial muscles are subcutaneous (just under the skin) muscles that control facial expression.
Muscle	Muscle is the contractile tissue of animals and is derived from the mesodermal layer of embryonic germ cells. Muscle cells contain contractile filaments that move past each other and change the size of the cell. They are classified as skeletal, cardiac, or smooth Muscles.
Eclampsia	Eclampsia , an acute and life-threatening complication of pregnancy, is characterized by the appearance of tonic-clonic seizures, usually in a patient who had developed preEclampsia. Eclampsia excludes seizures and coma that happen during pregnancy but are due to preexisting or organic brain disorders. Eclampsia is a leading cause of maternal and perinatal mortality.
Ectopic pregnancy	An Ectopic pregnancy is a complication of pregnancy in which the fertilized ovum is developed in any tissue other than the uterine wall. Most ectopic pregnancies occur in the Fallopian tube (so-called tubal pregnancies), but implantation can also occur in the cervix, ovaries, and abdomen. The fetus produces enzymes that allow it to implant in varied types of tissues, and thus an embryo implanted elsewhere than the uterus can cause great tissue damage in its efforts to reach a sufficient supply of blood.
Hydatidiform mole	Molar pregnancy is an abnormal form of pregnancy, wherein a non-viable, fertilized egg implants in the uterus, and thereby converting normal pregnancy processes into pathological ones. It characterized by the presence of a Hydatidiform mole (or hydatid mole, mola hytadidosa). Molar pregnancies are categorized into partial and complete moles, depending on the amount of maternal tissue present: complete moles have no identifiable embryonic or fetal tissues and arise when an empty egg with no nucleus is fertilized by a normal sperm; in contrast, a partial mole occurs when a normal egg is fertilized by two spermatozoa.
Vaginal delivery	A spontaneous Vaginal delivery occurs when a pregnant woman goes into labor with or without use of drugs or techniques to induce labor, and delivers her baby in the normal manner, without forceps, vacuum extraction, or a cesarean section.

	Assisted Vaginal delivery occurs when a pregnant woman goes into labor with or without the use of drugs or techniques to induce labor, and requires the use of special instruments such as forceps or a vacuum extractor to deliver her baby vaginally.
Canal	Canals are man-made channels for water. There are two types of Canal: · Aqueduct Canals that are used for the conveyance and delivery of fresh water, for human consumption, agriculture, etc. · Waterway Canals that are navigable transportation Canals used for carrying ships and boats loaded with goods and people, often connected to existing lakes, rivers, or oceans. Included here are inter-ocean Canals such as the Suez Canal and the Panama Canal. The word `Canal` is also used for a city-Canal in Dutch cities.
Bulbourethral gland	A Bulbourethral gland is one of two small exocrine glands present in the reproductive system of human males. They are homologous to Bartholin`s glands in females. Bulbourethral glands are located posterior and lateral to the membranous portion of the urethra at the base of the penis, between the two layers of the fascia of the urogenital diaphragm, in the deep perineal pouch.
Penis	The Penis (plural Penises, penes) is an external sexual organ of certain biologically male organisms, in both vertebrates and invertebrates. The Penis is a reproductive organ, technically an intromittent organ, and for placental mammals, additionally serves as the external organ of urination. The Penis is generally found on mammals and reptiles.
Prostate glands	The prostate is a compound tubuloalveolar exocrine gland of the male reproductive system in most mammals. Females do not have Prostate glands. A gland in females with similar characteristics to the prostate, previously called paraurethral or Skene`s glands, connected to the distal third of the urethra in the prevaginal space has been considered by a few researchers as a `prostate-like` gland.

Chapter 2. PART II: Chapter 5 - Chapter 8

Scrotum	In some male mammals the Scrotum is a protuberance of skin and muscle containing the testicles. It is an extension of the abdomen, and is located between the penis and anus. In humans and some other mammals, the base of the Scrotum becomes covered with curly pubic hairs at puberty.
Urethra	In anatomy, the Urethra is a tube which connects the urinary bladder to the outside of the body. In males, the Urethra travels through the penis, and carries semen as well as urine. In females, the Urethra is shorter and emerges above the vaginal opening.
Vas deferens	The Vas deferens , also called ductus deferens is part of the male anatomy of many vertebrates; they transport sperm from the epididymis in anticipation of ejaculation.
	There are two such ducts, connecting the left and right epididymis to the ejaculatory ducts in order to move sperm. Each tube is about 30 centimeters long (in humans) and is muscular (surrounded by smooth muscle).
Gland	A gland is an organ in an animal`s body that synthesizes a substance for release such as hormones or breast milk, often into the bloodstream (endocrine gland) or into cavities inside the body or its outer surface (exocrine gland).
	glands can be divided into 3 groups:
	· Endocrine glands -- are glands that secrete their products through the basal lamina and lack a duct system.
	· Exocrine glands -- secrete their products through a duct or directly onto the apical surface, the glands in this group can be divided into three groups:
	· Apocrine glands -- a portion of the secreting cell`s body is lost during secretion. Apocrine gland is often used to refer to the apocrine sweat glands, however it is thought that apocrine sweat glands may not be true apocrine glands as they may not use the apocrine method of secretion.
	· Holocrine glands -- the entire cell disintegrates to secrete its substances (e.g., sebaceous glands)

· Merocrine glands -- cells secrete their substances by exocytosis (e.g., mucous and serous glands). Also called `eccrine.`

The type of secretory product of an Exocrine gland may also be one of three categories:

· Serous glands -- secrete a watery, often protein-rich product.

· Mucous glands -- secrete a viscous product, rich in carbohydrates (e.g., glycoproteins).

· Sebaceous glands -- secrete a lipid product.
the third type; mixed

Every gland is formed by an ingrowth from an epithelial surface.

Major	Major is a rank of commissioned officer, with corresponding ranks existing in almost every military in the world.
	When used unhyphenated, in conjunction with no other indicator of rank, the term refers to the rank just senior to that of an Army captain and just below the rank of lieutenant colonel. It is considered the most junior of the field ranks.
Chordee	Chordee is a condition in which the head of the penis curves downward (that is, in a ventral direction) or upward, at the junction of the head and shaft of the penis. The curvature is usually most obvious during erection, but resistance to straightening is often apparent in the flaccid state as well. In many cases but not all, Chordee is associated with hypospadias.
Epididymis	The Epididymis is part of the male reproductive system and is present in all male amniotes. It is a narrow, tightly-coiled tube connecting the efferent ducts from the rear of each testicle to its vas deferens. A similar, but probably non-homologous, structure is found in cartilaginous fishes.
	The Epididymis can be divided into three main regions

· The head .

Maxilla	The maxilla , also known as the mustache bone, is a fusion of two bones along the palatal fissure that form the upper jaw. This is similar to the mandible , which is also a fusion of two halves at the mental symphysis. Sometimes (e.g. in bony fish), the maxilla is sometimes called `upper maxilla`, with the mandible being the `lower maxilla`.
Meatotomy	A Meatotomy is a form of penile modification in which the underside of the glans is split. The procedure may be performed by a doctor to alleviate meatal stenosis or urethral stricture, or by a body modification practitioner for the purpose of sexual pleasure or aesthetics. A Meatotomy can also result from a Prince Albert piercing being torn out.
Orchiopexy	Orchiopexy is a surgery to move an undescended testicle into the scrotum and permanently fix it there. It is performed by a pediatric urologist or surgeon on boys with cryptorchidism, typically before they reach the age of two. Some patients remain undiagnosed until their teenage years and undergo the surgery at that time.
Priapism	Priapism is a potentially harmful and painful medical condition in which the erect clitoris or penis does not return to its flaccid state, despite the absence of both physical and psychological stimulation, within four hours. Priapism is considered a medical emergency, which should receive proper treatment by a qualified medical practitioner. The name comes from the Greek god Priapus, referring to the myth that he was punished by the other gods for attempting to rape a goddess, by being given a massive, but useless, set of wooden genitals.
Tumescence	Tumescence is the quality or state of being tumescent or swollen. Tumescence usually refers to the normal engorgement with blood (vascular congestion) of the erectile tissues, marking sexual excitation and possible readiness for sexual activity. The tumescent sexual organ in men is the penis and in women is the clitoris.
Varicocele	Varicocele is an abnormal enlargement of the vein that is in the scrotum draining the testicles. The testicular blood vessels originate in the abdomen and course down through the inguinal canal as part of the spermatic cord on their way to the testis. Up-ward flow of blood in the veins is ensured by small one-way valves that prevent backflow.

Chapter 2. PART II: Chapter 5 - Chapter 8

Vasectomy	Vasectomy is a minor surgical procedure wherein the vasa deferentia of a man are severed, and then tied or sealed in a manner such to prevent sperm from entering the seminal stream (ejaculate).
	Typically done in an outpatient setting, a traditional Vasectomy involves numbing (local anesthetic) of the scrotum after which 1 (or 2) small incisions are made, allowing a surgeon to gain access to the vas deferens. The `tubes` are cut and sealed by tying, stitching, cauterization (burning), or otherwise clamped to prevent sperm from entering the seminal stream.
Vasovasostomy	Vasovasostomy (literally connection of the vas to the vas) is the surgery by which vasectomies are reversed in males. It can be performed in the convoluted or straight portion of the vas deferens.
	The medical term used to describe the reversal procedure is called Vasovasostomy (a form of microsurgery first performed by Earl Owen in 1971).
Cryptorchidism	Cryptorchidism is the absence of one or both testes from the scrotum. This usually represents failure of the testis to move, or `descend,` during fetal development from an abdominal position, through the inguinal canal, into the ipsilateral scrotum. About 3% of full-term and 30% of premature infant boys are born with at least one undescended testis, making Cryptorchidism the most common birth defect of male genitalia.
Epididymitis	Epididymitis is a medical condition in which there is inflammation of the epididymis (a curved structure at the back of the testicle in which sperm matures and is stored). This condition may be mildly to very painful, and the scrotum (sac containing the testicles) may become red, warm and swollen. It may be acute (of sudden onset) or rarely chronic.
Orchitis	Orchitis or Orchiditis is an often very painful condition of the testes involving inflammation, swelling and frequent infection. Symptoms of Orchitis are similar to those of testicular torsion. These can include: · ejaculation of blood · hematuria (blood in the urine)

	· severe pain
	· visible swelling of a testicle or testicles and often the inguinal lymph nodes on the affected side.
Pathophysiology	Pathophysiology is the study of the changes of normal mechanical, physical, and biochemical functions, either caused by a disease, or resulting from an abnormal syndrome. More formally, it is the branch of medicine which deals with any disturbances of body functions, caused by disease or prodromal symptoms.
	An alternate definition is `the study of the biological and physical manifestations of disease as they correlate with the underlying abnormalities and physiological disturbances.`
	The study of pathology and the study of Pathophysiology often involves substantial overlap in diseases and processes, but pathology emphasizes direct observations, while Pathophysiology emphasizes quantifiable measurements.
Hydrocele	A Hydrocele denotes a pathological accumulation of serous fluid in a bodily cavity.
	· A Hydrocele testis is the accumulation of fluids around a testicle, and is fairly common. A Hydrocele testis is due to fluid secreted from a remnant piece of peritoneum wrapped around the testis, called the tunica vaginalis.
Esophagus	The layers of the esophagus are as follows:
	· mucosa (mucus)
	· nonkeratinized stratified squamous epithelium: is rapidly turned over, and serves a protective effect due to the high volume transit of food, saliva and mucus.
	· lamina propria: sparse.
	· muscularis mucosae: smooth muscle

· submucosa: Contains the mucous secreting glands (esophageal glands), and connective structures termed papillae.

· muscularis externa (or `muscularis propria`): composition varies in different parts of the esophagus, to correspond with the conscious control over swallowing in the upper portions and the autonomic control in the lower portions:

· upper third, or superior part: striated muscle

· middle third, smooth muscle and striated muscle

· inferior third: predominantly smooth muscle

· adventitia
The junction between the esophagus and the stomach (the gastroesophageal junction or GE junction) is not actually considered a valve, although it is sometimes called the cardiac sphincter, cardia or cardias, although it is actually better resembles a stricture.

In most fish, the esophagus is extremely short, primarily due to the length of the pharynx (which is associated with the gills). However, some fish, including lampreys, chimaeras, and lungfish, have no true stomach, so that the oesophagus effectively runs from the pharynx directly to the intestine, and is therefore somewhat longer.

Epispadias	An Epispadias is a rare type of malformation of the penis in which the urethra ends in an opening on the upper aspect (the dorsum) of the penis. It occurs in around 1 in 120,000 male and 1 in 500,000 female births. Epispadias is an uncommon and partial form of a spectrum of failures of abdominal and pelvic fusion in the first months of embryogenesis known as the exstrophy - Epispadias complex.
Hypospadias	Hypospadias is a birth defect of the urethra in the male that involves an abnormally placed urinary meatus (opening). Instead of opening at the tip of the glans of the penis, a hypospadic urethra opens anywhere along a line (the urethral groove) running from the tip along the underside (ventral aspect) of the shaft to the junction of the penis and scrotum or perineum. A distal Hypospadias may be suspected even in an uncircumcised boy from an abnormally formed foreskin and downward tilt of the glans.
Urethritis	Urethritis is inflammation of the urethra. The main symptom is dysuria, which is painful or difficult urination.

Go to **Cram101.com** for Interactive Practice Exams for this book or virtually any of your books.
And, **NEVER** highlight a book again!

	Usually, the patient undresses and puts on a gown.
Balanitis	Balanitis is inflammation of the glans penis . When the foreskin is also affected, it is termed balanoposthitis. Balanitis on boys still in diapers must be distinguished from the normal redness seen in boys caused by ammoniacal dermatitis.
Phimosis	Phimosis (fÄ«-mÅ `sÄs, fÄ-), from the Greek phimos), is a condition where, in men, the male foreskin cannot be fully retracted from the head of the penis. The term may also refer to clitoral Phimosis in women, whereby the clitoral hood cannot be retracted, limiting exposure of the glans clitoris. In the neonatal period, it is rare for the foreskin to be retractable; Huntley et al.
Paraphimosis	Paraphimosis is a medical condition where the foreskin becomes trapped behind the glans penis, and cannot be pulled back to its normal flaccid position covering the glans penis. If the condition persists for several hours or there is any sign of a lack of blood flow, Paraphimosis should be treated as a medical emergency, as it can result in gangrene or other serious complications. Paraphimosis can often be reduced by manipulation.
Prostatitis	Prostatitis is an inflammation of the prostate gland, in men. A Prostatitis diagnosis is assigned at 8% of all urologist and 1% of all primary care physician visits in the United States. The term Prostatitis refers, in its strictest sense, to histological (microscopic) inflammation of the tissue of the prostate gland, although it is loosely (and confusingly) used to describe several completely different conditions.
Acute prostatitis	Men with this disease often have chills, fever, pain in the lower back and genital area, urinary frequency and urgency often at night, burning or painful urination, body aches, and a demonstrable infection of the urinary tract, as evidenced by white blood cells and bacteria in the urine. Acute prostatitis may be a complication of prostate biopsy. Acute prostatitis is relatively easy to diagnose due to its symptoms that suggest infection.
Prostate cancer	Prostate cancer is a form of cancer that develops in the prostate, a gland in the male reproductive system. The cancer cells may metastasize (spread) from the prostate to other parts of the body, particularly the bones and lymph nodes. Prostate cancer may cause pain, difficulty in urinating, problems during sexual intercourse, or erectile dysfunction.

Chapter 2. PART II: Chapter 5 - Chapter 8

Urinary system	The Urinary system is the organ system that produces, stores, and eliminates urine. In humans it includes two kidneys, two ureters, the bladder, the urethra, and the penis in males. The analogous organ in invertebrates is the nephridium.
Ureters	In human anatomy, the Ureters are muscular tubes that propel urine from the kidneys to the urinary bladder. In the adult, the Ureters are usually 25-30 cm (10-12 in) long and ~3-4 mm in diameter. In humans, the Ureters arise from the renal pelvis on the medial aspect of each kidney before descending towards the bladder on the front of the psoas major muscle.
Urinary bladder	In anatomy, the Urinary bladder is the organ that collects urine excreted by the kidneys prior to disposal by urination. A hollow muscular, and distensible (or elastic) organ, the bladder sits on the pelvic floor. Urine enters the bladder via the ureters and exits via the urethra.
Cystoscopy	Endoscopy of the urinary bladder via the urethra is called Cystoscopy. Diagnostic Cystoscopy is usually carried out with local anaesthesia. General anaesthesia is sometimes used for operative cystoscopic procedures.
Dysuria	In medicine, specifically urology, Dysuria refers to painful urination. Difficult urination is also sometimes described as Dysuria. It is one of a constellation of irritative bladder symptoms, which includes urinary frequency and haematuria.
Endometrium	The Endometrium is the inner membrane of the mammalian uterus. The Endometrium functions as a lining for the uterus, preventing adhesions between the opposed walls of the myometrium, thereby maintaining the patency of the uterine cavity. During the menstrual cycle or estrous cycle, the Endometrium grows to a thick, blood vessel-rich, glandular tissue layer.
Extracorporeal	An Extracorporeal medical procedure is a medical procedure which is performed outside the body.

A procedure in which blood is taken from a patient`s circulation to have a process applied to it before it is returned to the circulation. All of the apparatus carrying the blood outside the body is termed the Extracorporeal circuit.

· Hemodialysis

· Hemofiltration

· Plasmapheresis

· Apheresis

· Extracorporeal membrane oxygenation (ECMO)

· Cardiopulmonary bypass during open heart surgery.

Nephron	Nephron is the basic structural and functional unit of the kidney. Its chief function is to regulate the concentration of water and soluble substances like sodium salts by filtering the blood, reabsorbing what is needed and excreting the rest as urine. A nephron eliminates wastes from the body, regulates blood volume and blood pressure, controls levels of electrolytes and metabolites, and regulates blood pH. Its functions are vital to life and are regulated by the endocrine system by hormones such as antidiuretic hormone, aldosterone, and parathyroid hormone.
Nephrostomy	A Nephrostomy is an artificial opening created between the kidney and the skin which allows for the drainage of urine directly from the upper part of the urinary system (renal pelvis). A Nephrostomy is performed whenever a blockage keeps urine from passing from the kidneys, through the ureter and into the urinary bladder. Without another way for urine to drain, pressure would rise within the urinary system and the kidneys would be damaged.
Ureterolysis	Ureterolysis is a surgical procedure aimed at exposing the ureter in order to free it from external pressure or adhesions or to avoid injury to it during pelvic surgery, most often hysterectomy. The procedure can be done during open or laparoscopic surgery.
Urethropexy	A Urethropexy is a surgical procedure where support is provided to the urethra.

	One form is the `Burch Urethropexy`. It is sometimes performed in the treatment of incontinence (particularly stress incontinence).
Renal failure	Renal failure or kidney failure is a situation in which the kidneys fail to function adequately. It is divided into acute and chronic forms; either form may be due to a large number of other medical problems. Biochemically, it is typically detected by an elevated serum creatinine.
Cystitis	Cystitis is inflammation of the urinary bladder. The condition more often affects women, but can affect either sex and all age groups. There are several types of Cystitis: · Traumatic Cystitis is probably the most common form of Cystitis in the female, and is due to bruising of the bladder, usually by sexual intercourse.
Urinary tract infection	A Urinary tract infection is a bacterial infection that affects any part of the urinary tract. Although urine contains a variety of fluids, salts, and waste products, it usually does not have bacteria in it. When bacteria get into the bladder or kidney and multiply in the urine, they cause a Urinary tract infection. The most common type of Urinary tract infection is a bladder infection which is also often called cystitis.
Infection	An Infection is the detrimental colonization of a host organism by a foreign species. In an Infection, the infecting organism seeks to utilize the host`s resources to multiply, usually at the expense of the host. The infecting organism, or pathogen, interferes with the normal functioning of the host and can lead to chronic wounds, gangrene, loss of an infected limb, and even death.
Pyelonephritis	Pyelonephritis is an ascending urinary tract infection that has reached the pyelum (pelvis) of the kidney . If the infection is severe, the term `urosepsis` is used interchangeably . It requires antibiotics as therapy, and treatment of any underlying causes to prevent recurrence.

Chapter 2. PART II: Chapter 5 - Chapter 8

Glomerulonephritis	Glomerulonephritis, also known as glomerular nephritis, abbreviated GN, is a renal disease characterized by inflammation of the glomeruli, or small blood vessels in the kidneys. It may present with isolated hematuria and/or proteinuria (blood resp. protein in the urine); or as a nephrotic syndrome, a nephritic syndrome, acute renal failure, or chronic renal failure.
Nephrotic syndrome	Nephrotic syndrome is a nonspecific disorder in which the kidneys are damaged, causing them to leak large amounts of protein (proteinuria at least 3.5 grams per day per $1.73m^2$ body surface area) from the blood into the urine. Kidneys affected by Nephrotic syndrome have small pores in the podocytes, large enough to permit proteinuria but not large enough to allow cells through (hence no hematuria). By contrast, in nephritic syndrome, RBCs pass through the pores, causing hematuria.
Kidney stones	Kidney stones , are solid concretions formed in the kidneys from dissolved urinary minerals. The terms nephrolithiasis and urolithiasis refer to the condition of having calculi in the kidneys and urinary tract, respectively. Bladder stones can form or pass into the urinary bladder.
Nephrolithiasis	Kidney stones or renal calculi are solid concretions or calculi formed in the kidneys from dissolved urinary minerals. nephrolithiasis) refers to the condition of having kidney stones. Urolithiasis refers to the condition of having calculi in the urinary tract (which also includes the kidneys), which may form or pass into the urinary bladder.
Obstructive uropathy	Obstructive uropathy is a structural or functional hindrance of normal urine flow, sometimes leading to renal dysfunction (obstructive nephropathy). It is a very broad term, and does not imply a location or etiology. It can be caused by a lesion at any point in the urinary tract.
Osteoarthritis	Osteoarthritis (OA, also known as degenerative arthritis, degenerative joint disease), is a group of diseases and mechanical abnormalities entailing degradation of joints, including articular cartilage and the subchondral bone next to it. Clinical symptoms of OA may include joint pain, tenderness, stiffness, inflammation, creaking, and locking of joints. In OA, a variety of potential forces--hereditary, developmental, metabolic, and mechanical--may initiate processes leading to loss of cartilage -- a strong protein matrix that lubricates and cushions the joints.
Arteriole	An Arteriole is a small diameter blood vessel in the microcirculation that extends and branches out from an artery and leads to capillaries.

Arterioles have thin muscular walls (usually only one to two layers of smooth muscle) and are the primary site of vascular resistance. Arterioles receive autonomic nervous system innervation and respond to various circulating hormones in order to regulate their diameter.

Obstruction	Obstruction is the act of blocking or impeding some performance

· Obstruction theory, in mathematics

· Obstruction of justice, the crime of interfering with law enforcement

· Obstructing government administration

· Propagation path Obstruction

· Single Vegetative Obstruction Model

· Obstructive jaundice

· Obstructive sleep apnea

· Airway Obstruction, a respiratory problem

· Recurrent airway Obstruction

· Bowel Obstruction, a blockage of the intestines.

· Gastric outlet Obstruction

· Distal intestinal Obstruction syndrome

· Congenital lacrimal duct Obstruction

· Obstruction, when a fielder illegally hinders a baserunner

	· Obstructing the field
	· The Five Obstructions, a 2003 film
	· Obstruction Island (Washington)
	· Emergency Workers (Obstruction) Act 2006
Hydronephrosis	Hydronephrosis is distention and dilation of the renal pelvis and calyces, usually caused by obstruction of the free flow of urine from the kidney, leading to progressive atrophy of the kidney.
	The signs and symptoms of Hydronephrosis depend upon whether the obstruction is acute or chronic, partial or complete, unilateral or bilateral. Unilateral Hydronephrosis may occur without any symptoms, while acute obstruction can cause intense pain.
Polycystic kidney disease	Polycystic kidney disease is a cystic genetic disorder of the kidneys.
	It occurs in humans and other animals. Polycystic kidney disease is characterized by the presence of multiple cysts (hence, `polycystic`) in both kidneys.
Vascular	Vascular in zoology and medicine means `related to blood vessels`, which are part of the circulatory system. An organ or tissue that is Vascularized is heavily endowed with blood vessels and thus richly supplied with blood.
	In botany, plants with a dedicated transport system for water and nutrients are called Vascular plants.
Sacrum	The Sacrum is a large, triangular bone at the base of the spine and at the upper and back part of the pelvic cavity, where it is inserted like a wedge between the two hip bones. Its upper part connects with the last lumbar vertebra, and bottom part with the coccyx (tailbone). In children, it consists of usually five unfused vertebrae which begin to fuse between ages 16-18 and are usually completely fused into a single bone by age 26.
Salivary gland	

· Parasympathetic innervation to the Salivary glands is carried via cranial nerves. The parotid gland receives its parasympathetic input from the glossopharyngeal nerve (CN IX) via the otic ganglion, while the submandibular and sublingual glands receive their parasympathetic input from the facial nerve (CN VII) via the submandibular ganglion.

· Direct sympathetic innervation of the Salivary glands takes place via preganglionic nerves in the thoracic segments T1-T3 which synapse in the superior cervical ganglion with postganglionic neurons that release norepinephrine, which is then received by β-adrenergic receptors on the acinar and ductal cells of the Salivary glands, leading to an increase in cyclic adenosine monophosphate (cAMP) levels and the corresponding increase of saliva secretion.

Teeth	Teeth are small, calcified, whitish structures found in the jaws (or mouths) of many vertebrates that are used to tear, scrape, and chew food. Some animals, particularly carnivores, also use Teeth for hunting or defense. The roots of Teeth are covered by gums.
Pharynx	The pharynx is the part of the neck and throat situated immediately posterior to the mouth and nasal cavity, and cranial, or superior, to the esophagus, larynx, and trachea.
	The pharynx is part of the digestive system and respiratory system of many organisms.
	Because both food and air pass through the pharynx, a flap of connective tissue called the epiglottis closes over the trachea when food is swallowed to prevent choking or aspiration.
Sternum	The Sternum is a long flat bone shaped like a capital `T` located in the center of the thorax (chest). It connects to the rib bones via cartilage, forming the anterior section of the rib cage with them, and thus helps to protect the lungs, heart and major blood vessels from physical trauma.
	The Sternum is sometimes cut open (a median sternotomy) to gain access to the thoracic contents when performing cardiothoracic surgery.
Stomach	The stomach is a hollow muscular,sac-shaped digestive organ. between the esophagus and the small intestine. It is involved in the second phase of digestion, following mastication (chewing).

Chapter 2. PART II: Chapter 5 - Chapter 8

Family	Family is a group of people or animals (many species form the equivalent of a human Family wherein the adults care for the young) affiliated by consanguinity, affinity or co-residence. Although the concept of consanguinity originally referred to relations by `blood`, anthropologists have argued that one must understand the idea of `blood` metaphorically and that many societies understand Family through other concepts rather than through genetic distance. One of the primary functions of the Family is to produce and reproduce persons, biologically and socially.
Cecum	The Cecum or caecum is a pouch, connecting the ileum with the ascending colon of the large intestine. It is separated from the ileum by the ileocecal valve or Bauhin`s valve, and is considered to be the beginning of the large intestine. It is also separated from the colon by the cecocolic junction.
Colon	The colon is the last part of the digestive system in most vertebrates; it extracts water and salt from solid wastes before they are eliminated from the body, and is the site in which flora-aided (largely bacteria) fermentation of unabsorbed material occurs. Unlike the small intestine, the colon does not play a major role in absorption of foods and nutrients. However, the colon does absorb water, potassium and some fat soluble vitamins.
Duodenum	The Duodenum is the first section of the small intestine in most higher vertebrates, including mammals, reptiles, and birds. In fish, the divisions of the small intestine are not as clear and the terms anterior intestine or proximal intestine may be used instead of Duodenum. In mammals the Duodenum may be the principal site for iron absorption.
Gallbladder	The Gallbladder is a small non-vital organ that aids in the digestive process and stores bile produced in the liver. The Gallbladder is a hollow organ that sits in a concavity of the liver known as the Gallbladder fossa. In adults, the Gallbladder measures approximately 8 cm in length and 4 cm in diameter when fully distended.
Jejunum	The Jejunum is the middle section of the small intestine in most higher vertebrates, including mammals, reptiles, and birds. In fish, the divisions of the small intestine are not as clear and the terms middle intestine or mid-gut may be used instead of Jejunum. The Jejunum lies between the duodenum and the ileum.

CRAM101

Large intestine	The large intestine is the second to last part of the digestive system--the final stage of the alimentary canal is the anus --in vertebrate animals. Its function is to absorb water from the remaining indigestible food matter, and then to pass useless waste material from the body
Liver	The liver is a vital organ present in vertebrates and some other animals. It has a wide range of functions, including detoxification, protein synthesis, and production of biochemicals necessary for digestion. The liver is necessary for survival; there is currently no way to compensate for the absence of liver function.
Palatine	A Palatine or palatinus was a high-level official attached to imperial or royal courts in Europe since Roman times. The term palatinus was first used in Ancient Rome for chamberlains of the Emperor due to their association with the Palatine Hill, the imperial palace guard after the rise of Constantine I were also called the Scholae Palatinae for the same reason. In the Early Middle Ages the title became attached to courts beyond the imperial one; the highest level of officials in the Roman Catholic Church were called the judices palatini.
Palatine tonsils	Palatine tonsils, occasionally called the faucial tonsils, are the tonsils that can be seen on the left and right sides at the back of the throat. Tonsillitis is an inflammation of the tonsils and will often, but not necessarily, cause a sore throat and fever. In chronic cases tonsillectomy may be indicated.
Pancreas	The pancreas is a gland organ in the digestive and endocrine system of vertebrates. It is both an endocrine gland producing several important hormones, including insulin, glucagon, and somatostatin, as well as an exocrine gland, secreting pancreatic juice containing digestive enzymes that pass to the small intestine. These enzymes help in the further breakdown of the carbohydrates, protein, and fat in the chyme.
Peritoneum	The Peritoneum is the serous membrane that forms the lining of the abdominal cavity or the coelom -- it covers most of the intra-abdominal (or coelomic) organs -- in higher vertebrates and some invertebrates (annelids, for instance). It is composed of a layer of mesothelium supported by a thin layer of connective tissue. The Peritoneum both supports the abdominal organs and serves as a conduit for their blood and lymph vessels and nerves.
Sigmoid	Sigmoid means resembling the lower-case Greek letter sigma (ς). Specific uses include: · Sigmoid function, a mathematical function

217

	· Sigmoid colon, part of the large intestine or colon
Small intestine	In vertebrates, the small intestine is the part of the gastrointestinal tract (gut) following the stomach and followed by the large intestine, and is where the vast majority of digestion and absorption of food takes place. In invertebrates such as worms, the terms `gastrointestinal tract` and `large intestine` are often used to describe the entire intestine
Intestine	In anatomy, the Intestine is the segment of the alimentary canal extending from the stomach to the anus and, in humans and other mammals, consists of two segments, the small Intestine and the large Intestine. In humans, the small Intestine is further subdivided into the duodenum, jejunum and ileum while the large Intestine is subdivided into the cecum and colon. The structure and function can be described both as gross anatomy and at a microscopic level.
Tonsils	The Tonsils are areas of lymphoid tissue on either side of the throat. An infection of the Tonsils is called tonsillitis. Most commonly, the term `Tonsils` refers to the palatine Tonsils that can be seen in the back of the throat.
Anastomosis	An Anastomosis is a network of streams that both branch out and reconnect, such as blood vessels or leaf veins. The term is used in medicine, biology, mycology and geology.
Cholangiography	Cholangiography is the imaging of the bile duct (also known as the biliary tree) by x-rays. There are at least two kinds of Cholangiography: · percutaneous transhepatic Cholangiography (PTC): Examination of liver and bile ducts by x-rays. This is accomplished by the insertion of a thin needle into the liver carrying a contrast medium to help to see blockage in liver and bile ducts.
Cholecystectomy	Cholecystectomy is the surgical removal of the gallbladder. It is the most common method for treating symptomatic gallstones. Surgical options include the standard procedure, called laparoscopic Cholecystectomy, and an older more invasive procedure, called open Cholecystectomy.

Chapter 2. PART II: Chapter 5 - Chapter 8

Colonoscopy	Colonoscopy is the endoscopic examination of the large colon and the distal part of the small bowel with a CCD camera or a fibre optic camera on a flexible tube passed through the anus. It may provide a visual diagnosis (e.g. ulceration, polyps) and grants the opportunity for biopsy or removal of suspected lesions. Virtual Colonoscopy, which uses 2D and 3D imagery reconstructed from computed tomography (CT) scans or from nuclear magnetic resonance (MR) scans, is also possible, as a totally non-invasive medical test, although it is not standard and still under investigation regarding its diagnostic abilities.
Colostomy	A Colostomy is a surgical procedure that involves connecting a part of the colon onto the anterior abdominal wall, leaving the patient with an opening on the abdomen called a stoma. In a Colostomy, the stoma is formed from the end of the large intestine, which is drawn out through the incision and sutured to the skin. After a Colostomy, feces leave the patient`s body through the abdomen.
Diverticulum	A Diverticulum is medical or biological term for an outpouching of a hollow (or a fluid filled) structure in the body. In medicine the term usually implies that the structure is not normally present, i.e., pathological. However, in the embryonic stage, some normal structures begin development as a Diverticulum arising from another structure. An alphabetical listing of some frequently encountered diverticula follows: · Bladder Diverticulum: Balloon-like growths on the bladder commonly associated with a chronic outflow obstruction, such as benign prostatic hyperplasia in older males.
Dysphagia	Dysphagia is the medical term for the symptom of difficulty in swallowing. Although classified under `symptoms and signs` in ICD-10, the term is sometimes used as a condition in its own right. Sufferers are sometimes unaware of their Dysphagia.
Evisceration	Evisceration is the removal of viscera, (internal organs, especially those in the abdominal cavity). This can refer to: · disembowelment, removal of the internal organs of an animal or person.

	· Evisceration (autotomy), ejection of viscera as a defensive action by an animal.
Frontal bone	The Frontal bone is a bone in the human skull that resembles a cockleshell in form, and consists of two portions:
	· a vertical portion, the squama frontalis, corresponding with the region of the forehead.
	· an orbital or horizontal portion, the pars orbitalis, which enters into the formation of the roofs of the orbital and nasal cavities.
	The Frontal bone is presumed to be derived from neural crest cells.
	The border of the squama frontalis is thick, strongly serrated, bevelled at the expense of the inner table above, where it rests upon the parietal bones, and at the expense of the outer table on either side, where it receives the lateral pressure of those bones; this border is continued below into a triangular, rough surface, which articulates with the great wing of the sphenoid.
Gastrostomy	Gastrostomy refers to a surgical opening into the stomach. Creation of an artificial external opening into the stomach for nutritional support or gastrointestinal compression. Typically this would include an incision in the patient's epigastrium as part of a formal operation.
Hernia	A Hernia is a protrusion of a tissue, structure, or part of an organ through the muscle tissue or the membrane by which it is normally contained. The Hernia has three parts: the orifice through which it Herniates, the Hernial sac, and its contents. By far the most common Hernias develop in the abdomen, when a weakness in the abdominal wall evolves into a localized hole, or `defect`, through which adipose tissue, or abdominal organs covered with peritoneum, may protrude.
Ileostomy	An Ileostomy is a stoma that has been constructed by bringing the end or loop of small intestine (the ileum) out onto the surface of the skin. Intestinal waste passes out of the Ileostomy and is collected in an external pouching system stuck to the skin. Ileostomies are usually sited above the groin on the right hand side of the abdomen.

Chapter 2. PART II: Chapter 5 - Chapter 8

Intussusception	An intussusception is a medical condition in which a part of the intestine has invaginated into another section of intestine, similar to the way in which the parts of a collapsible telescope slide into one another. This can often result in an obstruction. The part that prolapses into the other is called the intussusceptum, and the part that receives it is called the intussuscipiens.
Lithotomy	Lithotomy from Greek for `lithos` and `tomos` (cut), is a surgical method for removal of calculi, stones formed inside certain hollow organs, such as the bladder and kidneys (urinary calculus) and gallbladder (gallstones), that cannot exit naturally through the urethra, ureter or biliary duct. The procedure, which is usually done by means of a surgical incision (therefore invasive), differs from lithotripsy, wherein the stones are crushed either by a minimally invasive probe inserted through the exit canal, or by ultrasound waves (extracorporeal lithotripsy), which is a non-invasive procedure. Human beings have known of bladder stones (`vesical calculi`) for thousands of years, and have attempted to treat them for almost as long.
Lithotripsy	Extracorporeal Shock Wave Lithotripsy is the non-invasive treatment of kidney stones (urinary calculosis) and biliary calculi (stones in the gallbladder or in the liver) using an acoustic pulse. Lithotripsy and the lithotriptor were developed in the early 1980s in Germany by Dornier Medizintechnik GmbH , and came into widespread use with the introduction of the HM-3 lithotriptor in 1983. Within a few years, ESWL became a standard treatment of calculosis. It is estimated that more than one million patients are treated annually with ESWL in the USA alone.
Heart	The Heart is a muscular organ found in most vertebrates that is responsible for pumping blood throughout the blood vessels by repeated, rhythmic contractions. The term cardiac (as in cardiology) means `related to the Heart` and comes from the Greek καρδίη, kardia, for `Heart.` The vertebrate Heart is composed of cardiac muscle, an involuntary striated muscle tissue which is found only within this organ. The average human Heart, beating at 72 beats per minute, will beat approximately 2.5 billion times during a lifetime (about 66 years).
Hepatitis	Hepatitis (plural hepatitides) implies injury to the liver characterized by the presence of inflammatory cells in the tissue of the organ. The name is from ancient Greek hepar , the root being hepat- (á¼¡πατ-), meaning liver, and suffix -itis, meaning `inflammation` (c. 1727).
Hepatitis E	Hepatitis E is a viral hepatitis (liver inflammation) caused by infection with a virus called Hepatitis E virus (HEV). HEV is a positive-sense single-stranded RNA icosahedral virus with a 7.5 kilobase genome. HEV has a fecal-oral transmission route.

Prolactin	Prolactin or Luteotropic hormone (LTH) is a peptide hormone discovered by Dr. Henry Friesen, primarily associated with lactation. In breastfeeding, the act of an infant suckling the nipple stimulates the production of Prolactin, which fills the breast with milk via a process called lactogenesis, in preparation for the next feed. Oxytocin, another hormone, is also released, which triggers milk let-down.
Volvulus	A Volvulus is a bowel obstruction in which a loop of bowel has abnormally twisted on itself. · Volvulus Neonatorum · Volvulus Small Intestine · Volvulus Caecum · Volvulus Sigmoid Colon Midgut Volvulus occurs in patients (usually in infants) that are predisposed because of congenital intestinal malrotation. Segmental Volvulus occurs in patients of any age, usually with a predisposition because of abnormal intestinal contents (e.g. meconium ileus) or adhesions. Volvulus of the cecum, transverse colon, or sigmoid colon occurs, usually in adults, with only minor predisposing factors such as redundant (excess, inadequately supported) intestinal tissue and constipation.
Aphthous ulcer	An Aphthous ulcer also known as a canker sore, is a type of oral ulcer, which presents as a painful open sore inside the mouth or upper throat characterized by a break in the mucous membrane. Its cause is unknown. The condition is also known as aphthous stomatitis, and alternatively as Sutton's Disease, especially in the case of major, multiple, or recurring ulcers.
Cleft palate	Cleft lip (cheiloschisis) and Cleft palate (colloquially known as harelip), which can also occur together as cleft lip and palate, are variations of a type of clefting congenital deformity caused by abnormal facial development during gestation. A cleft is a fissure or opening--a gap. It is the non-fusion of the body's natural structures that form before birth.
Esophagitis	Esophagitis is inflammation of the esophagus. · The most common cause is gastroesophageal reflux disease . If caused by GERD, the diseases is also called reflux Esophagitis.

	· Other causes of Esophagitis include infections (most commonly candida, herpes simplex and cytomegalovirus). These infections are typically seen in immunocompromised people, such as those with HIV. · Chemical injury by alkaline or acid solutions may also cause Esophagitis, and is usually seen in children, as well as in adults who attempt suicide by ingestion of caustic substances · Physical injury resulting from radiation therapy or by nasogastric tubes may also be responsible. · Hyperacidity. · Alcohol abuse. · Eosinophilic Esophagitis is a little understood form of Esophagitis, which is thought to be related to food allergies.
Herpes simplex	Herpes simplex is a viral disease caused by both Herpes simplex virus 1 (HSV-1) and Herpes simplex virus 2 (HSV-2). Infection with the herpes virus is categorized into one of several distinct disorders based on the site of infection. Oral herpes, the visible symptoms of which are colloquially called cold sores, infects the face and mouth.
Herpes simplex virus	Herpes simplex virus 1 and 2 (Herpes simplex virus-1 and Herpes simplex virus-2), also known as Human herpes virus 1 and 2 (HHV-1 and -2), are two members of the herpes virus family, Herpesviridae, that infect humans. Both Herpes simplex virus-1 and -2 are ubiquitous and contagious. They can be spread when an infected person is producing and shedding the virus.
Progressive systemic sclerosis	Progressive systemic sclerosis is a generalized disorder of connective tissue in which there is thickening of dermal collagen bundles, and fibrosis and vascular abnormalities in internal organs.
Scleroderma	Scleroderma is a chronic autoimmune disease characterized by fibrosis , vascular alterations, and autoantibodies. There are two major forms: Limited cutaneous Scleroderma (or morphea) mainly affects the hands, arms and face, although pulmonary hypertension is frequent. Diffuse cutaneous Scleroderma (or systemic sclerosis) is rapidly progressing and affects a large area of the skin and one or more internal organs, frequently the kidneys, esophagus, heart and lungs, and can be fatal.
Sarcoma	A Sarcoma is a cancer of the connective tissue resulting in mesoderm proliferation.

	This is in contrast to carcinomas, which are of epithelial origin (breast, colon, pancreas, and others). However, due to an evolving understanding of tissue origin, the term `Sarcoma` is sometimes applied to tumors now known to arise from epithelial tissue.
Diaphragmatic hernia	Diaphragmatic hernia is a defect or hole in the diaphragm that allows the abdominal contents to move into the chest cavity. Treatment is usually surgical. The following types of Diaphragmatic hernia exist: · Congenital Diaphragmatic hernia · Morgagni`s hernia · Bochdalek hernia · Hiatal hernia · Iatrogenic Diaphragmatic hernia · Traumatic Diaphragmatic hernia A scaphoid abdomen (sucked inwards) may be the presenting symptom in a newborn.
Gastritis	Gastritis is an inflammation of the lining of the stomach, and has many possible causes. The main acute causes are excessive alcohol consumption or prolonged use of nonsteroidal anti-inflammatory drugs (also known as NSAIDs) such as aspirin or ibuprofen. Sometimes Gastritis develops after major surgery, traumatic injury, burns, or severe infections.
Gastroesophageal reflux disease	Gastroesophageal reflux disease (GERD), gastro-oesophageal reflux disease (GORD), gastric reflux disease, or acid reflux disease is defined as chronic symptoms or mucosal damage produced by the abnormal reflux in the esophagus. This is commonly due to transient or permanent changes in the barrier between the esophagus and the stomach. This can be due to incompetence of the lower esophageal sphincter, transient lower esophageal sphincter relaxation, impaired expulsion of gastric reflux from the esophagus, or a hiatal hernia.

Chapter 2. PART II: Chapter 5 - Chapter 8

Atrophic gastritis	Atrophic gastritis (also known as Type A Gastritis) is a process of chronic inflammation of the stomach mucosa, leading to loss of gastric glandular cells and their eventual replacement by intestinal and fibrous tissues. As a result, the stomach's secretion of essential substances such as hydrochloric acid, pepsin, and intrinsic factor is impaired, leading to digestive problems, vitamin B12 deficiency, and megaloblastic anemia. It can be caused by persistent infection with Helicobacter pylori, or can be autoimmune in origin.
Superficial	Superficial is an adjective generally meaning 'regarding the surface', often metaphorically. Both in the literal as in the metaphorical sense the term has often a negative connotation based on the idea that deeper parts are also important to consider. · In human anatomy, Superficial describes objects near the body's surface as compared to other objects that may be deep. For example, skin is a Superficial structure of the body and muscles are deep to skin.
Peptic ulcer	A Peptic ulcer PUD or Peptic ulcer disease, is an ulcer (defined as mucosal erosions equal to or greater than 0.5 cm) of an area of the gastrointestinal tract that is usually acidic and thus extremely painful. As many as 80% of ulcers are associated with Helicobacter pylori, a spiral-shaped bacterium that lives in the acidic environment of the stomach, however only 40% of those cases go to a doctor. Ulcers can also be caused or worsened by drugs such as aspirin and other NSAIDs.
Pyloric stenosis	Pyloric stenosis is a condition that causes severe vomiting in the first few months of life. There is narrowing (stenosis) of the opening from the stomach to the intestines, due to enlargement (hypertrophy) of the muscle surrounding this opening (the pylorus, meaning 'gate'), which spasms when the stomach empties. It is uncertain whether there is a real congenital narrowing or whether there is a functional hypertrophy of the muscle which develops in the first few weeks of life.
Stenosis	A Stenosis is an abnormal narrowing in a blood vessel or other tubular organ or structure. It is also sometimes called a 'stricture' . The term 'coarctation' is synonymous, but is commonly used only in the context of aortic coarctation.

Chapter 2. PART II: Chapter 5 - Chapter 8

Enteritis	In medicine, Enteritis refers to inflammation of the small intestine. It is most commonly caused by the ingestion of substances contaminated with pathogenic microorganisms. Symptoms include abdominal pain, cramping, diarrhea, dehydration and fever.
Appendicitis	Appendicitis is a condition characterized by inflammation of the appendix. It is a medical emergency. All cases require removal of the inflamed appendix, either by laparotomy or laparoscopy.
Peritonitis	Peritonitis is defined as inflammation of the peritoneum (the serous membrane which lines part of the abdominal cavity and some of the viscera it contains). It may be localised or generalised, generally has an acute course, and may depend on either infection (often due to rupture of a hollow organ as may occur in abdominal trauma) or on a non-infectious process. The main manifestations of Peritonitis are acute abdominal pain, abdominal tenderness, and abdominal guarding, which are exacerbated by moving the peritoneum, e.g. coughing (forced cough may be used as a test), flexing one's hips, or eliciting the Blumberg sign (a.k.a. rebound tenderness, meaning that pressing a hand on the abdomen elicits less pain than releasing the hand abruptly, which will aggravate the pain, as the peritoneum snaps back into place).
Diverticulosis	Diverticulosis, otherwise known as 'diverticular disease,' is the condition of having diverticula in the colon, which are outpocketings of the colonic mucosa and submucosa through weaknesses of muscle layers in the colon wall. These are more common in the sigmoid colon, which is a common place for increased pressure. This is uncommon before the age of 40 for some unknown reason Diverticulosis is being treated in patients as young as 35 years old, and increases in incidence after that age.
Diverticulitis	Diverticulitis is a common digestive disease particularly found in the large intestine. Diverticulitis develops from diverticulosis, which involves the formation of pouches (diverticula) on the outside of the colon. Diverticulitis results if one of these diverticula becomes inflamed.
Ulcerative colitis	Ulcerative colitis (Colitis ulcerosa, Ulcerative colitis) is a form of inflammatory bowel disease (IBD). Ulcerative colitis is a form of colitis, a disease of the intestine, specifically the large intestine or colon, that includes characteristic ulcers, or open sores, in the colon. The main symptom of active disease is usually constant diarrhea mixed with blood, of gradual onset.
Colitis	Colitis is a chronic digestive disease characterized by inflammation of the colon. Colitis is one of a group of conditions which are inflammatory and auto-immune, affecting the tissue that lines the gastrointestinal system (the large and small intestine). It is classed as an inflammatory bowel disease (IBD), not to be confused with irritable bowel syndrome (IBS).

Chapter 2. PART II: Chapter 5 - Chapter 8

Colorectal cancer	Colorectal cancer, also called colon cancer or large bowel cancer, includes cancerous growths in the colon, rectum and appendix. With 655,000 deaths worldwide per year, it is the fourth most common form of cancer in the United States and the third leading cause of cancer-related death in the Western world. Colorectal cancers arise from adenomatous polyps in the colon.
Hepatitis A	Hepatitis A is an acute infectious disease of the liver caused by the Hepatitis A virus (HAV), which is most commonly transmitted by the fecal-oral route via contaminated food or drinking water. Every year, approximately 10 million people worldwide are infected with the virus. The time between infection and the appearance of the symptoms, (the incubation period), is between two and six weeks and the average incubation period is 28 days.
Jaundice	Jaundice, also known as icterus (attributive adjective: icteric), is a yellowish discoloration of the skin, the conjunctival membranes over the sclerae (whites of the eyes), and other mucous membranes caused by hyperbilirubinemia (increased levels of bilirubin in the blood). This hyperbilirubinemia subsequently causes increased levels of bilirubin in the extracellular fluids. Typically, the concentration of bilirubin in the plasma must exceed 1.5 mg/dL, three times the usual value of approximately 0.5mg/dL, for the coloration to be easily visible.
Vestibule	Vestibule or Vestibulum can have the following meanings, each primarily based upon a common origin, from early 17th century French, derived from Latin vestibulum, -i n. `entrance court`. In general, Vestibule is a small space or cavity at the beginning of a canal. · a covered section between the outer opening and inner opening of a tent, typically used for the storage of boots, packs and small equipment. · The Vestibules , a Canadian comedy troupe · Teh Vestibule, an IGN message board · Vestibulum (wasp), a wasp genus `
Viral	The term Viral is used to describe anything related to viruses.

	Viral may also mean:
	˙ .
Viral hepatitis	Viral hepatitis is liver inflammation due to a viral infection. It may present in acute (recent infection, relatively rapid onset) or chronic forms. The most common causes of Viral hepatitis are the five unrelated hepatotropic viruses Hepatitis A, Hepatitis B, Hepatitis C, Hepatitis D, and Hepatitis E. In addition to the hepatitis viruses, other viruses that can also cause hepatitis include Cytomegalovirus, Epstein-Barr virus, and Yellow fever.
Hepatitis B	Hepatitis B is a disease caused by Hepatitis B virus (HBV) which infects the liver of hominoidae, including humans, and causes an inflammation called hepatitis. Originally known as `serum hepatitis`, the disease has caused epidemics in parts of Asia and Africa, and it is endemic in China. About a third of the world`s population, more than 2 billion people, have been infected with the Hepatitis B virus.
Hepatitis D	Hepatitis D, also referred to as Hepatitis D virus (HDV) and classified as Hepatitis Delta virus, is a disease caused by a small circular RNA virus. HDV is considered to be a subviral satellite because it can propagate only in the presence of the Hepatitis B virus (HBV). Transmission of HDV can occur either via simultaneous infection with HBV (coinfection) or via infection of an individual previously infected with HBV (superinfection).
Cirrhosis	Cirrhosis is a consequence of chronic liver disease characterized by replacement of liver tissue by fibrous scar tissue as well as regenerative nodules (lumps that occur as a result of a process in which damaged tissue is regenerated), leading to progressive loss of liver function. Cirrhosis is most commonly caused by alcoholism, hepatitis B and C, and fatty liver disease but has many other possible causes. Some cases are idiopathic, i.e., of unknown cause.
Cholangitis	Cholangitis is inflammation of the bile duct. The most common cause is a bacterial infection, and the problem is then an ascending Cholangitis. However, there are other types of Cholangitis as well.
Cholecystitis	Cholecystitis is inflammation of the gall bladder. Cholecystitis is often caused by cholelithiasis (the presence of choleliths, or gallstones, in the gallbladder), with choleliths most commonly blocking the cystic duct directly. This leads to inspissation (thickening) of bile, bile stasis, and secondary infection by gut organisms, predominantly E. coli and Bacteroides species.

Gallstone	In medicine, Gallstones (choleliths) are crystalline bodies formed within the body by accretion or concretion of normal or abnormal bile components.
	Gallstones can occur anywhere within the biliary tree, including the gallbladder and the common bile duct. Obstruction of the common bile duct is choledocholithiasis; obstruction of the biliary tree can cause jaundice; obstruction of the outlet of the pancreatic exocrine system can cause pancreatitis.
Pancreatitis	Pancreatitis is inflammation of the pancreas that can occur in two very different forms. Acute Pancreatitis is sudden while chronic Pancreatitis `is characterized by recurring or persistent abdominal pain with or without steatorrhea or diabetes mellitus.`
	Excessive alcohol use is often cited as the most common cause of acute Pancreatitis, yet gallstones are actually the most common cause. Less common causes include hypertriglyceridemia (but not hypercholesterolemia) and only when triglyceride values exceed 1500 mg/dl (16 mmol/L), hypercalcemia, viral infection (e.g., mumps), trauma (to the abdomen or elsewhere in the body) including post-ERCP (i.e., Endoscopic Retrograde Cholangiopancreatography), vasculitis (i.e., inflammation of the small blood vessels within the pancreas), and autoimmune Pancreatitis.
Pancreatic cancer	Pancreatic cancer is a malignant neoplasm of the pancreas. Each year in the United States, about 42,470 individuals are diagnosed with this condition and 35,240 die from the disease. The prognosis is relatively poor but has improved; the three-year survival rate is now about thirty percent, but less than 5 percent of those diagnosed are still alive five years after diagnosis.

Mediastinum	The Mediastinum is a non-delineated group of structures in the thorax, surrounded by loose connective tissue. It is the central compartment of the thoracic cavity. It contains the heart, the great vessels of the heart, esophagus, trachea, phrenic nerve, cardiac nerve, thoracic duct, thymus, and lymph nodes of the central chest.
Lymph	Lymph is the interstitial fluid found between the cells of the human body. It enters the Lymph vessels by filtration through pores in the walls of capillaries. The Lymph then travels to at least one Lymph node before emptying ultimately into the right or the left subclavian vein, where it mixes back with blood.
Lymphatic system	The Lymphatic system in vertebrates is a network of conduits that carry a clear fluid called lymph. It also includes the lymphoid tissue through which the lymph travels. Lymphoid tissue is found in many organs, particularly the lymph nodes, and in the lymphoid follicles associated with the digestive system such as the tonsils.
Vessels	Vessels are a post-rock band from Leeds, UK. Vessels were born from the ashes of A Day Left in September 2005. In 2006 the band self-released a five track eponymous EP, and played many gigs, including the unsigned stage at Leeds Festival as one of the six winners of the Futuresound competition. On 5 March 2007, the band released a limited 7` single (Yuki/Forever the Optimist) through Cuckundoo Records, and have been tipped by BBC Radio One as one of the hottest new bands in the country. The band recorded a session for Huw Stephens `s show on BBC Radio 1, which was broadcast on 29 March.
Axillary artery	In human anatomy, the Axillary artery is a large blood vessel that conveys oxygenated blood to the lateral aspect of the thorax, the axilla (armpit) and the upper limb. Its origin is at the lateral margin of the first rib, before which it is called the subclavian artery. After passing the lower margin of teres major it becomes the brachial artery.
Infundibulum	An Infundibulum is a funnel-shape cavity or organ. · Lungs: The alveolar sacs of the lungs from which the air chambers (alveoli) open are called infundibula

· Heart: The outflow portion of the right ventricle, the Infundibulum of the heart, is another name for the conus arteriosus

· Ovaries: The end of the mammal oviduct nearest to the ovary is the Infundibulum of uterine tube

· Brain: A small outgrowth of the ventral wall of the embryo brain from which the pars nervosa (the posterior lobe) of the pituitary gland develops is also called the Infundibulum. (Another name for this structure is the pituitary stalk).

· Kidney: Part of the collecting system in the kidneys; urine flows from the calyces, through the infundibula into the renal pelves

· Ethmoid bone: Ethmoidal Infundibulum

· In the science fiction novel The Sirens of Titan by Kurt Vonnegut a `chronosynclastic Infundibulum` is a kind of wormhole through time and space, defined as `where all the different kinds of truths fit together`

· Geometry The arc of a sphere or any portion of a circle

Lymph node	A Lymph node is a small bean-shaped organ of the immune system, distributed widely throughout the body and linked by lymphatic vessels. Lymph nodes are garrisons of B, T, and other immune cells. Lymph nodes are found all through the body, and act as filters or traps for foreign particles.
Lymphadenectomy	Lymphadenectomy consists of the surgical removal of one or more groups of lymph nodes. It is almost always performed as part of the surgical management of cancer. This is usually done because many types of cancer have a marked tendency to produce lymph node metastasis early on in their natural history.
Arteries	Arteries are blood vessels that carry blood away from the heart. All Arteries, with the exception of the pulmonary and umbilical Arteries, carry oxygenated blood. The circulatory system is extremely important for sustaining life.

Chapter 3. PART III: Chapter 9 - Chapter 13

Foramen	In anatomy, a Foramen is any opening. Many foramina transmit muscle or a nerve.
Leukemia	Leukemia is a cancer of the blood or bone marrow and is characterized by an abnormal proliferation (production by multiplication) of blood cells, usually white blood cells (leukocytes). Leukemia is a broad term covering a spectrum of diseases. In turn, it is part of the even broader group of diseases called hematological neoplasms.
Lymphangitis	Lymphangitis is an inflammation of the lymphatic channels that occurs as a result of infection at a site distal to the channel. The most common cause of Lymphangitis in humans is Streptococcus Pyogenes (Group A strep). Lymphangitis is also sometimes called `blood poisoning.`
	Lymphangitis is the inflammation of the lymphatic vessels/channels. This is characterized by certain inflammatory conditions of the skin caused by bacterial infections. Thin red lines may be observed running along the course of the lymphatic vessels in the affected area, accompanied by painful enlargement of the nearby lymph nodes.
Splenectomy	A Splenectomy is a surgical procedure that partially or completely removes the spleen.
	The spleen, similar in structure to a large lymph node, acts as a blood filter. Current knowledge of its purpose includes the removal of old red blood cells and platelets, and the detection and fight against certain bacteria.
Stem cell	Stem cells are cells found in most, if not all, multi-cellular organisms. They are characterized by the ability to renew themselves through mitotic cell division and differentiating into a diverse range of specialized cell types. Research in the Stem cell field grew out of findings by Canadian scientists Ernest A. McCulloch and James E. Till in the 1960s.
Thoracic duct	In human anatomy, the Thoracic duct is an important part of the lymphatic system--it is the largest lymphatic vessel in the body. It is also known under various other names including the alimentary duct, chyliferous duct, the left lymphatic duct and Van Hoorne's canal.

	It collects most of the lymph in the body and drains into the systemic (blood) circulation at the left brachiocephalic vein, right between where the left subclavian vein and left internal jugular connect.
Aorta	The Aorta is the largest artery in the body, originating from the left ventricle of the heart and extends down to the abdomen, where it branches off into two smaller arteries. The Aorta brings oxygenated blood to all parts of the body in the systemic circulation.

The Aorta is usually divided into five segments/sections:

· Ascending Aorta--the section between the heart and the arch of Aorta

· Arch of Aorta--the peak part that looks somewhat like an inverted 'U'

· Descending Aorta--the section from the arch of Aorta to the point where it divides into the common iliac arteries

· Thoracic Aorta--the half of the descending Aorta above the diaphragm

· Abdominal Aorta--the half of the descending Aorta below the diaphragm

All amniotes have a broadly similar arrangement to that of humans, albeit with a number of individual variations. In fish, however, there are two separate vessels referred to as Aortas. |
| Anemia | Anemia is a decrease in normal number of red blood cells or less than the normal quantity of hemoglobin in the blood. However, it can include decreased oxygen-binding ability of each hemoglobin molecule due to deformity or lack in numerical development as in some other types of hemoglobin deficiency.
Since hemoglobin (found inside RBCs) normally carries oxygen from the lungs to the tissues, Anemia leads to hypoxia (lack of oxygen) in organs. |
| Aplastic anemia | · Anaemia with malaise, pallor and associated symptoms such as palpitations |

· Thrombocytopenia (low platelet counts), leading to increased risk of hemorrhage, bruising and petechiae

· Leukopenia (low white blood cell count), leading to increased risk of infection

· Reticulocytopenia (low reticulocyte counts)
The condition needs to be differentiated from pure red cell aplasia. In Aplastic anemia the patient has pancytopenia (i.e., anemia, neutropenia and thrombocytopenia) resulting in decrease of all formed elements. In contrast, pure red cell aplasia is characterized by reduction in red cells only.

Iron deficiency	Iron deficiency is one of the most commonly known forms of nutritional deficiencies. In the human body, iron is present in all cells and has several vital functions--as a carrier of oxygen to the tissues from the lungs in the form of hemoglobin, as a transport medium for electrons within the cells in the form of cytochromes, and as an integral part of enzyme reactions in various tissues. Too little iron can interfere with these vital functions and lead to morbidity and mortality.
Deficiency	A Deficiency is a lack of something. Example

there is a Deficiency of oxygen in the air and we shall soon suffocate.

· In mathematics, a deficient number is a number n for which $\sigma(n) < 2n$.

· In medicine there are a variety of nutrient deficiencies:

· Avitaminosis is a Deficiency of vitamins.

· Boron Deficiency

· Chromium Deficiency

· Iron Deficiency |

· Iodine Deficiency

· Magnesium Deficiency

· Micronutrient Deficiency

· In construction, a Deficiency is an item, or condition that is considered sub-standard, or below minimum expectations, such as those mandated by either drawings or specifications or the building code or the fire code, and/or any combination of the foregoing. Deficiencies are routinely discussed and dealt with in construction site meetings.

· In genetics, a genetic deletion is also called a Deficiency.

· In real estate law, a Deficiency in the ability to pay off a debt is called a Deficiency judgment or Deficiency judgement.

Pathophysiology	Pathophysiology is the study of the changes of normal mechanical, physical, and biochemical functions, either caused by a disease, or resulting from an abnormal syndrome. More formally, it is the branch of medicine which deals with any disturbances of body functions, caused by disease or prodromal symptoms.
	An alternate definition is `the study of the biological and physical manifestations of disease as they correlate with the underlying abnormalities and physiological disturbances.`
	The study of pathology and the study of Pathophysiology often involves substantial overlap in diseases and processes, but pathology emphasizes direct observations, while Pathophysiology emphasizes quantifiable measurements.
Granulocytosis	In medicine, Granulocytosis is the presence in peripheral blood of an increased number of granulocytes, a category of white blood cells. Often, the word refers to an increased neutrophil granulocyte count, as neutrophils are the main granulocytes.
	An increase in eosinophil granulocyte is known as eosinophilia.

Granulocytosis can be a feature of a number of diseases:

· Infection, especially bacterial

· Malignancy, most notably leukemia (it is the main feature of chronic myelogenous leukemia, CML)

· Autoimmune disease
In cardiovascular disease, increased white blood cell counts have been shown to indicate a worse prognosis.

Hemolytic anemia	Hemolytic anemia is anemia due to hemolysis, the abnormal breakdown of red blood cells (RBCs) either in the blood vessels (intravascular hemolysis) or elsewhere in the body (extravascular). It has numerous possible causes, ranging from relatively harmless to life-threatening. The general classification of Hemolytic anemia is either acquired or inherited.
Basilic vein	In human anatomy, the Basilic vein is a large superficial vein of the upper limb that helps drain parts of hand and forearm. It originates on the medial (ulnar) side of the dorsal venous network of the hand, and it travels up the base of the forearm and arm. Most of its course is superficial; it generally travels in the subcutaneous fat and other fasciae that lie superficial to the muscles of the upper extremity.
Infectious mononucleosis	Infectious mononucleosis is an infectious, very widespread viral disease caused by the Epstein-Barr virus , a type of Herpes virus, which well over 90% of all adults are exposed to at some point in their lives. Most people are exposed to the virus as children, when the disease produces no noticeable symptoms or only flu-like symptoms. In underdeveloped countries, people are exposed to the virus in early childhood more often than in developed countries, which is why the disease in its observable form is more common in developed countries.
Monocytosis	Monocytosis is an increase in the number of monocytes circulating in the blood. Monocytes are white blood cells that give rise to macrophages and dendritic cells in the immune system. In humans, 950/µL is regarded as at the upper limit of normal; monocyte counts above this level are regarded as Monocytosis.

Chapter 3. PART III: Chapter 9 - Chapter 13

Disease	A Disease or medical condition is an abnormal condition of an organism that impairs bodily functions, associated with specific symptoms and signs. It may be caused by external factors, such as invading organisms, or it may be caused by internal dysfunctions, such as autoimmune Diseases. In human beings, `Disease` is often used more broadly to refer to any condition that causes pain, dysfunction, distress, social problems, and/or death to the person afflicted, or similar problems for those in contact with the person.
Lymphadenopathy	Lymphadenopathy is a term meaning `disease of the lymph nodes.` It is, however, almost synonymously used with `swollen/enlarged lymph nodes`. It could be due to infection, auto-immune disease, or malignancy. Inflammation of a lymph node is called lymphadenitis.
Accountability	Accountability is a concept in ethics and governance with several meanings. It is often used synonymously with such concepts as responsibility, answerability, blameworthiness, liability, and other terms associated with the expectation of account-giving. As an aspect of governance, it has been central to discussions related to problems in the public sector, nonprofit and private (corporate) worlds.
Health	At the time of the creation of the World Health Organization (WHO), in 1948, Health was defined as being `a state of complete physical, mental, and social well-being and not merely the absence of disease or infirmity`. This definition invited nations to expand the conceptual framework of their Health systems beyond issues related to the physical condition of individuals and their diseases, and it motivated us to focus our attention on what we now call social determinants of Health. Consequently, WHO challenged political, academic, community, and professional organizations devoted to improving or preserving Health to make the scope of their work explicit, including their rationale for allocating resources.
Health insurance	Health insurance is insurance that pays for medical expenses. It is sometimes used more broadly to include insurance covering disability or long-term nursing or custodial care needs. It may be provided through a government-sponsored social insurance program, or from private insurance companies.

Chapter 3. PART III: Chapter 9 - Chapter 13

Lymphoma	Lymphoma is a cancer that begins in the lymphocytes of the immune system and presents as a solid tumor of lymphoid cells. They often originate like balls in lymph nodes, presenting as an enlargement of the node (a tumor). Lymphomas are closely related to lymphoid leukemias, which also originate in lymphocytes but typically involve only circulating blood and the bone marrow and do not usually form static tumours.
Multiple myeloma	Multiple myeloma , also known as Multiple myeloma, myeloma, plasma cell myeloma,) is a cancer of the white blood cells known as plasma cells, which produce antibodies. These plasma cells, or B cells, are part of the immune system, formed in bone marrow, and numerous in lymphatics. Myeloma is incurable, but remissions may be induced with steroids, chemotherapy, thalidomide and stem cell transplants.
Plasma cell	Plasma cells, also called plasma B cells, plasmocytes, and effector B cells, are white blood cells that produce large volumes of antibodies. They are transported by the blood plasma and the lymphatic system. Like all blood cells, Plasma cells ultimately originate in the bone marrow; however, these cells leave the bone marrow as B cells, before terminal differentiation into Plasma cells, which usually happens in lymph nodes.
Cancer	Cancer is a genetic disorder in which the normal control of cell growth is lost. Cancer genetics is now one of the fastest expanding medical specialties. At the molecular level, Cancer is caused by mutation(s) in DNA, which result in aberrant cell proliferation.
Adrenocorticotropic hormone	Adrenocorticotropic hormone is a polypeptide tropic hormone produced and secreted by the anterior pituitary gland. It is an important component of the hypothalamic-pituitary-adrenal axis and is often produced in response to biological stress . Its principal effects are increased production of corticosteroids and, as its name suggests, cortisol from the adrenal cortex.
Endocardium	The Endocardium is the innermost layer of tissue that lines the chambers of the heart. Its cells are embryologically and biologically similar to the endothelial cells that line blood vessels. The Endocardium underlies the much more voluminous myocardium, the muscular tissue responsible for the contraction of the heart.
Endocrine glands	Endocrine glands are glands of the endocrine system that secrete their products, hormones, directly into the blood rather than through a duct. The main Endocrine glands include the pituitary gland, pancreas, ovaries, testes, thyroid gland, and adrenal glands. The hypothalamus is a neuroendocrine organ.

259

Endocrine system	The Endocrine system is a system of glands, each of which secretes a type of hormone to regulate the body. The field of study that deals with disorders of endocrine glands is endocrinology, a branch of the wider field of internal medicine. The Endocrine system is an information signal system much like the nervous system.
Pituitary gland	The pituitary gland, or hypophysis, is an endocrine gland about the size of a pea and weighing 0.5 g (0.02 oz).. It is a protrusion off the bottom of the hypothalamus at the base of the brain, and rests in a small, bony cavity (sella turcica) covered by a dural fold (diaphragma sellae). The pituitary fossa, in which the pituitary gland sits, is situated in the sphenoid bone in the middle cranial fossa at the base of the brain.
Gland	A gland is an organ in an animal`s body that synthesizes a substance for release such as hormones or breast milk, often into the bloodstream (endocrine gland) or into cavities inside the body or its outer surface (exocrine gland).
	glands can be divided into 3 groups:
	· Endocrine glands -- are glands that secrete their products through the basal lamina and lack a duct system.
	· Exocrine glands -- secrete their products through a duct or directly onto the apical surface, the glands in this group can be divided into three groups:
	· Apocrine glands -- a portion of the secreting cell`s body is lost during secretion. Apocrine gland is often used to refer to the apocrine sweat glands, however it is thought that apocrine sweat glands may not be true apocrine glands as they may not use the apocrine method of secretion.
	· Holocrine glands -- the entire cell disintegrates to secrete its substances (e.g., sebaceous glands)
	· Merocrine glands -- cells secrete their substances by exocytosis (e.g., mucous and serous glands). Also called `eccrine.`
	The type of secretory product of an Exocrine gland may also be one of three categories:

· Serous glands -- secrete a watery, often protein-rich product.

· Mucous glands -- secrete a viscous product, rich in carbohydrates (e.g., glycoproteins).

· Sebaceous glands -- secrete a lipid product.
the third type; mixed

Every gland is formed by an ingrowth from an epithelial surface.

Gland

A gland is an organ in an animal`s body that synthesizes a substance for release such as hormones or breast milk, often into the bloodstream (endocrine gland) or into cavities inside the body or its outer surface (exocrine gland).

glands can be divided into 3 groups:

· Endocrine glands -- are glands that secrete their products through the basal lamina and lack a duct system.

· Exocrine glands -- secrete their products through a duct or directly onto the apical surface, the glands in this group can be divided into three groups:

· Apocrine glands -- a portion of the secreting cell`s body is lost during secretion. Apocrine gland is often used to refer to the apocrine sweat glands, however it is thought that apocrine sweat glands may not be true apocrine glands as they may not use the apocrine method of secretion.

· Holocrine glands -- the entire cell disintegrates to secrete its substances (e.g., sebaceous glands)

· Merocrine glands -- cells secrete their substances by exocytosis (e.g., mucous and serous glands). Also called `eccrine.`
The type of secretory product of an Exocrine gland may also be one of three categories:

· Serous glands -- secrete a watery, often protein-rich product.

· Mucous glands -- secrete a viscous product, rich in carbohydrates (e.g., glycoproteins).

· Sebaceous glands -- secrete a lipid product.
the third type; mixed

Every gland is formed by an ingrowth from an epithelial surface.

Hormone	A Hormone is a chemical released by one or more cells that affects cells in other parts of the organism. Only a small amount of Hormone is required to alter cell metabolism. It is essentially a chemical messenger that transports a signal from one cell to another.
Antidiuretic	An Antidiuretic is an agent or drug that, administered to an organism, helps control body water balance by reducing urination, opposing diuresis.
	Antidiuretics are the drugs that reduce urine volume, particularly in diabetes insipidus (DI) which is their primary indication.
	These are classified as:
	· Antidiuretic hormones: ADH/Vasopressin, Desmopressin, Lypressin, Terlipressin
	· Miscellaneous: Chlorpropamide, Carbamazepine
Growth hormone	Growth hormone is a peptide hormone secreted by the pituitary gland that stimulates growth and cell reproduction. In the past Growth hormone was extracted from human pituitary glands. Growth hormone is now produced by recombinant DNA technology and is prescribed for a variety of reasons.
Luteinizing hormone	Luteinizing hormone is a hormone produced by the anterior pituitary gland.

· In the female, an acute rise of Luteinizing hormone - the Luteinizing hormone surge - triggers ovulation and corpus luteum development.

· In the male, where Luteinizing hormone had also been called Interstitial Cell Stimulating Hormone , it stimulates Leydig cell production of testosterone.
Luteinizing hormone is a heterodimeric glycoprotein. Each monomeric unit is a glycoprotein molecule; one alpha and one beta subunit make the full, functional protein.

Oxytocin	Oxytocin is a mammalian hormone that also acts as a neurotransmitter in the brain. It is best known for its roles in female reproduction: it is released in large amounts after distension of the cervix and vagina during labor, and after stimulation of the nipples, facilitating birth and breastfeeding, respectively. Recent studies have begun to investigate Oxytocin`s role in various behaviors, including orgasm, social recognition, pair bonding, anxiety, trust, love, and maternal behaviors.
Palatine	A Palatine or palatinus was a high-level official attached to imperial or royal courts in Europe since Roman times. The term palatinus was first used in Ancient Rome for chamberlains of the Emperor due to their association with the Palatine Hill, the imperial palace guard after the rise of Constantine I were also called the Scholae Palatinae for the same reason. In the Early Middle Ages the title became attached to courts beyond the imperial one; the highest level of officials in the Roman Catholic Church were called the judices palatini.
Palatine tonsils	Palatine tonsils, occasionally called the faucial tonsils, are the tonsils that can be seen on the left and right sides at the back of the throat. Tonsillitis is an inflammation of the tonsils and will often, but not necessarily, cause a sore throat and fever. In chronic cases tonsillectomy may be indicated.
Pancreas	The pancreas is a gland organ in the digestive and endocrine system of vertebrates. It is both an endocrine gland producing several important hormones, including insulin, glucagon, and somatostatin, as well as an exocrine gland, secreting pancreatic juice containing digestive enzymes that pass to the small intestine. These enzymes help in the further breakdown of the carbohydrates, protein, and fat in the chyme.

Parathyroid gland	The parathyroid glands are small endocrine glands in the neck that produce parathyroid hormone. Humans have four parathyroid glands, which are usually located behind the thyroid gland, and, in rare cases, within the thyroid gland or in the chest. parathyroid glands control the amount of calcium in the blood and within the bones.
Prolactin	Prolactin or Luteotropic hormone (LTH) is a peptide hormone discovered by Dr. Henry Friesen, primarily associated with lactation. In breastfeeding, the act of an infant suckling the nipple stimulates the production of Prolactin, which fills the breast with milk via a process called lactogenesis, in preparation for the next feed. Oxytocin, another hormone, is also released, which triggers milk let-down.
Thyroid	The thyroid is one of the largest endocrine glands in the body. This gland is found in the neck inferior to (below) the thyroid cartilage (also known as the Adam's apple in men) and at approximately the same level as the cricoid cartilage. The thyroid controls how quickly the body uses energy, makes proteins, and controls how sensitive the body should be to other hormones.
Thyroid-stimulating hormone	Thyroid-stimulating hormone is a peptide hormone synthesized and secreted by thyrotrope cells in the anterior pituitary gland, which regulates the endocrine function of the thyroid gland. TSH stimulates the thyroid gland to secrete the hormones thyroxine and triiodothyronine (T_3). TSH production is controlled by thyrotropin-releasing hormone (TRH), which is manufactured in the hypothalamus and transported to the anterior pituitary gland via the superior hypophyseal artery, where it increases TSH production and release.
Vasopressin	Arginine Vasopressin argipressin or antidiuretic hormone (ADH), is a hormone found in most mammals, including humans. Vasopressin is a peptide hormone which controls the reabsorbtion of molecules in the tubules of the kidneys by affecting the tissue's permeability. It plays a key role in homeostasis, and the regulation of water, glucose and salts in the blood.
Tonsils	The Tonsils are areas of lymphoid tissue on either side of the throat. An infection of the Tonsils is called tonsillitis. Most commonly, the term 'Tonsils' refers to the palatine Tonsils that can be seen in the back of the throat.
Hypothalamus	The Hypothalamus is a portion of the brain that contains a number of small nuclei with a variety of functions. One of the most important functions of the Hypothalamus is to link the nervous system to the endocrine system via the pituitary gland (hypophysis).

	The Hypothalamus is located below the thalamus, just above the brain stem.
Pineal gland	The Pineal gland is a small endocrine gland in the vertebrate brain. It produces melatonin, a hormone that affects the modulation of wake/sleep patterns and photoperiodic (seasonal) functions. It is shaped like a tiny pine cone (hence its name), and is located near the center of the brain, between the two hemispheres, tucked in a groove where the two rounded thalamic bodies join.
Placenta	The Placenta is an organ that connects the developing fetus to the uterine wall to allow nutrient uptake, waste elimination and gas exchange via the mother's blood supply. Placentas are a defining characteristic of eutherian or 'Placental' mammals, but are also found in some snakes and lizards with varying levels of development up to mammalian levels. The word Placenta comes from the Latin for cake, from Greek plakóenta/plakoúnta, accusative of plakóeis/plakoús - πλακΪŒεις, πλακοΪ ς, 'flat, slab-like', in reference to its round, flat appearance in humans.
Kidney	The Kidneys are paired organs, which have the production of urine as their primary function. Kidneys are seen in many types of animals, including vertebrates and some invertebrates. They are an essential part of the urinary system, but have several secondary functions concerned with homeostatic functions.
Isthmus	An Isthmus is a narrow strip of land connecting two larger land areas. Of note, the Isthmus of Corinth connects the peninsula of Peloponnese with the rest of the Greek peninsula, the Isthmus of Panama connects the continents of North and South America , and the Isthmus of Suez in Egypt connects Africa and Asia (or Eurasia). Canals are often built on Isthmuses where they may be particularly advantageous to create a shortcut for marine transportation.
Thyroglossal duct	The Thyroglossal duct is an embryological anatomical structure forming an open connection between the initial area of development of the thyroid gland and its final position. The thyroid gland starts developing in the oropharynx in the fetus and descends to its final position taking a path through the tongue, hyoid bone and neck muscles. The connection between its original position and its final position is the Thyroglossal duct.

Chapter 3. PART III: Chapter 9 - Chapter 13

Thyroidectomy	A Thyroidectomy is an operation that involves the surgical removal of all or part of the thyroid gland. Surgeons often perform a Thyroidectomy when a patient has thyroid cancer or some other condition of the thyroid gland (such as hyperthyroidism). Other indications for surgery include cosmetic (very enlarged thyroid), or symptomatic obstruction (causing difficulties in swallowing or breathing).
Diabetes	Diabetes mellitus --often referred to as diabetes--is a condition in which the body either does not produce enough, or does not properly respond to, insulin, a hormone produced in the pancreas. Insulin enables cells to absorb glucose in order to turn it into energy. This causes glucose to accumulate in the blood , leading to various potential complications. Many types of diabetes are recognized: The principal three are: · Type 1: Results from the body`s failure to produce insulin.
Acromegaly	Acromegaly is a syndrome that results when the pituitary gland produces excess growth hormone (hGH) after epiphyseal plate closure at puberty. A number of disorders may increase the pituitary's GH output, although most commonly it involves a GH producing tumor called pituitary adenoma, derived from a distinct type of cell (somatotrophs). Acromegaly most commonly affects adults in middle age, and can result in severe disfigurement, serious complicating conditions, and premature death if unchecked.
Dwarfism	Dwarfism is short stature resulting from an abnormal medical condition. It is sometimes defined as an adult height of less than 4 feet 10 inches (147 cm), although this definition is problematic because short stature in itself is not a disease. Dwarfism can be caused by over 200 distinct medical conditions, such that the symptoms and characteristics of individual dwarfs vary greatly.
Gestational diabetes	Gestational diabetes (, Gestational diabetesM) is a condition in which women without previously diagnosed diabetes exhibit high blood glucose levels during pregnancy.

	Gestational diabetes generally has few symptoms and it is most commonly diagnosed by screening during pregnancy. Diagnostic tests detect inappropriately high levels of glucose in blood samples.
Hypopituitarism	Hypopituitarism is the decreased (hypo) secretion of one or more of the eight hormones normally produced by the pituitary gland at the base of the brain. If there is decreased secretion of most pituitary hormones, the term panHypopituitarism (pan meaning `all`) is used. The signs and symptoms of Hypopituitarism vary, depending on which hormones are undersecreted and on the underlying cause of the abnormality.
Diabetes insipidus	Diabetes insipidus is a condition characterized by excessive thirst and excretion of large amounts of severely diluted urine, with reduction of fluid intake having no effect on the latter. There are several different types of Diabetes insipidus, each with a different cause. The most common type is neurogenic Diabetes insipidus, caused by a deficiency of arginine vasopressin (AVP), also known as antidiuretic hormone (ADH).
Hyperthyroidism	Hyperthyroidism is the term for overactive tissue within the thyroid gland causing an overproduction of thyroid hormones (thyroxine or `T4` and/or triiodothyronine or `T3`). Hyperthyroidism is thus a cause of thyrotoxicosis, the clinical condition of increased thyroid hormones in the blood. It is important to note that Hyperthyroidism and thyrotoxicosis are not synonymous.
Cretinism	Cretinism is a condition of severely stunted physical and mental growth due to untreated congenital deficiency of thyroid hormones (congenital hypothyroidism) due to maternal nutritional deficiency of iodine.
	The term cretin describes a person so affected, but, like words such as spastic and lunatic, also is a word of abuse. Cretin became a medical term in the 18th century, from an Alpine French dialect prevalent in a region where persons with such a condition were especially common ; it saw wide medical use in the 19th and early 20th centuries, and then spread more widely in popular English as a markedly derogatory term for a person who behaves stupidly.
Hypothyroidism	Hypothyroidism is the disease state in humans and in animals caused by insufficient production of thyroid hormone by the thyroid gland. Cretinism is a form of Hypothyroidism found in infants.
	About three percent of the general population is hypothyroidic.

Chapter 3. PART III: Chapter 9 - Chapter 13

Hard palate	The Hard palate is a thin horizontal bony plate of the skull, located in the roof of the mouth. It spans the arch formed by the upper teeth.
	It is formed by the palatine process of the maxilla and horizontal plate of palatine bone.
Hyperparathyroidism	Hyperparathyroidism is overactivity of the parathyroid glands resulting in excess production of parathyroid hormone (PTH). The parathyroid hormone regulates calcium and phosphate levels and helps to maintain these levels. Excessive PTH secretion may be due to problems in the glands themselves, in which case it is referred to as primary hyperparathryroidism and which leads to hypercalcemia (raised calcium levels).
Hypoparathyroidism	In medicine (endocrinology), Hypoparathyroidism is decreased function of the parathyroid glands, leading to decreased levels of parathyroid hormone (PTH). The consequence, hypocalcaemia, is a serious medical condition.
	· Tingling lips, fingers, and toes
	· Muscle cramps
	· Pain in the face, legs, and feet
	· Abdominal pain
	· Dry hair
	· Brittle nails
	· Dry, scaly skin
	· Cataracts
	· Weakened tooth enamel (in children)
	· Muscle spasms called tetany (can lead to spasms of the larynx, causing breathing difficulties)

· Convulsions (seizures)

· Tetanic contractions
Additional symptoms that may be associated with this disease include:

· Painful menstruation

· Hand or foot spasms

· Decreased consciousness

· Delayed or absent tooth formation
In contrast to hyperparathyroidism (hyperfunction of the parathyroids), Hypoparathyroidism does not have consequences for bone.

Diagnosis is by measurement of calcium, serum albumin (for correction) and PTH in blood.

Thyroiditis	Thyroiditis is the inflammation of the thyroid gland. The thyroid gland is located on the front of the neck below the laryngeal prominence, and makes hormones that control metabolism.
	There are many different types of Thyroiditis, with the most common being Hashimoto`s Thyroiditis.
Adrenal glands	In mammals, the adrenal glands are the star-shaped endocrine glands that sit on top of the kidneys. They are chiefly responsible for releasing hormones in conjunction with stress through the synthesis of corticosteroids and catecholamines, including cortisol and adrenaline (epinephrine), respectively.
	Anatomically, the adrenal glands are located in the retroperitoneum situated atop the kidneys, one on each side.

CTam101

Chapter 3. PART III: Chapter 9 - Chapter 13

Syndrome	In medicine and psychology, the term syndrome refers to the association of several clinically recognizable features, signs (observed by a physician), symptoms (reported by the patient), phenomena or characteristics that often occur together, so that the presence of one feature alerts the physician to the presence of the others. In recent decades the term has been used outside of medicine to refer to a combination of phenomena seen in association. The term syndrome derives from its Greek roots and means literally `run together`, as the features do.
Adrenal medulla	The Adrenal medulla is part of the adrenal gland. It is located at the center of the gland, being surrounded by the adrenal cortex. The Adrenal medulla consists of irregularly shaped cells grouped around blood vessels.
Hyperaldosteronism	Hyperaldosteronism, also aldosteronism, is a medical condition where too much aldosterone is produced by the adrenal glands, which can lead to lowered levels of potassium in the blood. In endocrinology, the terms primary and secondary are used to describe the abnormality (e.g., elevated aldosterone) in relation to the defect, i.e., the tumor`s location.  · E26.0: Primary aldosteronism, Primary Hyperaldosteronism was previously thought to be most commonly caused by an adrenal adenoma, termed Conn`s syndrome.
Medulla	Medulla refers to the middle of something and derives from the Latin word for marrow. Its anatomical uses include: · Medulla oblongata, a part of the brain stem · Renal Medulla, a part of the kidney · Adrenal Medulla, a part of the adrenal gland · Medulla ossea, the marrow inside a bone

· Medulla spinalis, an alternative name for the spinal cord

· Medulla of ovary

· Medulla of thymus

· Medulla of lymph node

· Medulla
Non-medical uses of the term include:

· Medúlla, a 2004 music album by Icelandic singer Björk

· Medulla, Florida, a U.S. city

· Las Médulas, Ancient Roman gold mines in León, Spain

· Medulla Grammatice Grammaticae, a fifteenth-century Latin-Middle English dictionary `

Androgen	Androgen, also called Androgenic hormones or testoids, is the generic term for any natural or synthetic compound, usually a steroid hormone, that stimulates or controls the development and maintenance of male characteristics in vertebrates by binding to Androgen receptors. This includes the activity of the accessory male sex organs and development of male secondary sex characteristics. Androgens were first discovered in 1936. Androgens are also the original anabolic steroids and the precursor of all estrogens, the female sex hormones.
Estrogen	Estrogens (U.S., otherwise oEstrogens or Å"strogens) are a group of steroid compounds and functioning as the primary female sex hormone, their name comes from estrus/oistros (period of fertility for female mammals) + gen/gonos = to generate. Estrogens are used as part of some oral contraceptives, in Estrogen replacement therapy for postmenopausal women, and in hormone replacement therapy for trans women.

	Like all steroid hormones, Estrogens readily diffuse across the cell membrane.
Astrocytes	Astrocytes are characteristic star-shaped glial cells in the brain and spinal cord. They perform many functions, including biochemical support of endothelial cells which form the blood-brain barrier, provision of nutrients to the nervous tissue, maintenance of extracellular ion balance, and a principal role in the repair and scarring process of the brain and spinal cord following traumatic injuries. Research since the mid-1990s has shown that Astrocytes propagate intercellular Ca^{2+} waves over long distances in response to stimulation, and, similar to neurons, release transmitters (called gliotransmitters) in a Ca^{2+}-dependent manner.
Microglia	Microglia are a type of glial cells that are the resident macrophages of the brain and spinal cord, and thus act as the first and main form of active immune defense in the central nervous system (CNS). Microglia constitute 20% of the total glial cell population within the brain. Microglia are distributed in large non-overlapping regions throughout the brain and spinal cord.
Nervous system	The Nervous system is an organ system containing a network of specialized cells called neurons that coordinate the actions of an animal and transmit signals between different parts of its body. In most animals the Nervous system consists of two parts, central and peripheral. The central Nervous system contains the brain and spinal cord.
Neuron	A neuron is an electrically excitable cell that processes and transmits information by electrochemical signaling, via connections with other cells called synapses. neurons are the core components of the nervous system, which includes the brain, spinal cord, and peripheral ganglia. A number of specialized types of neurons exist: sensory neurons respond to touch, sound, light and numerous other stimuli affecting cells of the sensory organs that then send signals to the spinal cord and brain.
Central nervous system	The Central nervous system is the part of the nervous system that functions to coordinate the activity of all parts of the bodies of multicellular organisms. In vertebrates, the Central nervous system is enclosed in the meninges. It contains the majority of the nervous system and consists of the brain and the spinal cord.
Brainstem	The Brainstem is the lower part of the brain, adjoining and structurally continuous with the spinal cord. The Brainstem provides the main motor and sensory innervation to the face and neck via the cranial nerves. Though small, this is an extremely important part of the brain as the nerve connections of the motor and sensory systems from the main part of the brain to the rest of the body pass through the brain stem.

285

Cephalic vein	In human anatomy, the Cephalic vein is a superficial vein of the upper limb.
	It communicates with the basilic vein via the median cubital vein at the elbow and is located in the superficial fascia along the anterolateral surface of the biceps brachii muscle.
	Superiorly the Cephalic vein passes between the deltoid and pectoralis major muscles (deltopectoral groove) and through the deltopectoral triangle, where it empties into the axillary vein.
Cerebellum	The Cerebellum is a region of the brain that plays an important role in motor control. It is also involved in some cognitive functions such as attention and language, and probably in some emotional functions such as regulating fear and pleasure responses, but its function in movement is the most clearly understood. The Cerebellum does not initiate movement, but it contributes to coordination, precision, and accurate timing.
Cerebrum	

Parietal lobe
Occipital lobe
Temporal lobe
Interlobar

	sulci/fissures
Limbic lobe Insular lobe General Some categorizations are approximations, and some Brodmann areas span gyri. The lobes of the cerebral cortex include the frontal (blue), temporal (green), occipital (red), and parietal lobes (yellow). The cerebellum (unlabeled) is not part of the telencephalon. Diagram depicting the main subdivisions of the embryonic vertebrate brain.	
Artery	anterior cerebral, middle cerebral, posterior cerebral
Vein	cerebral veins
MeSH	Telencephalon
NeuroLex ID	birnlex_1042
	The Cerebrum or telencephalon, together with the diencephalon, constitute the forebrain. It is the most anterior or, especially in humans, most superior region of the vertebrate central nervous system.
Diencephalon	The Diencephalon is the region of the brain that includes the thalamus, metathalamus, hypothalamus, epithalamus, prethalamus or subthalamus and pretectum. It combines with the telencephalon to form the prosencephalon (forebrain). The Diencephalon is located near the midline of the brain, above the mesencephalon (midbrain).

Peripheral nervous system	The peripheral nervous system resides or extends outside the central nervous system (CNS), which consists of the brain and spinal cord. The main function of the peripheral nervous system is to connect the CNS to the limbs and organs. Unlike the central nervous system, the peripheral nervous system is not protected by bone or by the blood-brain barrier, leaving it exposed to toxins and mechanical injuries.
Pons	The Pons is a structure located on the brain stem. It is cranial to (up from) the medulla oblongata, caudal to (down from) the midbrain, and ventral to (in front of) the cerebellum. In humans and other bipeds this means it is above the medulla, below the midbrain, and anterior to the cerebellum.
Spinal cord	The Spinal cord is a long, thin, tubular bundle of nervous tissue and support cells that extends from the brain. The brain and Spinal cord together make up the central nervous system. The Spinal cord extends down to the space in between the first and second lumbar vertebrae.
Autonomic nervous system	The Autonomic nervous system is the part of the peripheral nervous system that acts as a control system functioning largely below the level of consciousness, and controls visceral functions. The Autonomic nervous system affects heart rate, digestion, respiration rate, salivation, perspiration, diameter of the pupils, micturition (urination), and sexual arousal. Whereas most of its actions are involuntary, some, such as breathing, work in tandem with the conscious mind.
Sympathetic	The word Sympathetic means different things in different contexts. · In neurology and neuroscience, the Sympathetic nervous system is a part of the autonomic nervous system. · In music theory, Sympathetic strings are strings on a musical instrument that resonate without contact. · In psychology, sympathy is a feeling of compassion or identification with another. · In religion, magic, and anthropology, sympathy is the belief that like affects like, that something can be influenced through its relationship with another thing.

Craniotomy	A Craniotomy is a surgical operation in which a bone flap is removed from the skull, to access the brain. Craniotomies are often a critical operation performed on patients suffering from brain lesions or traumatic brain injury (TBI), and can also allow doctors to surgically implant deep brain stimulators for the treatment of Parkinson's disease, epilepsy and cerebellar tremor. The procedure is also widely used in neuroscience for extracellular recording, brain imaging, and for neurological manipulations such as electrical stimulation and chemical titration.
Cranium	The skull is a bony structure found in the head of many animals. The skull supports the structures of the face and protects the head against injury. The skull can be divided into two parts: the Cranium and the mandible.
Discectomy	A Discectomy is a surgical procedure in which the central portion of an intervertebral disc, the nucleus pulposus, which is causing pain by stressing the spinal cord or radiating nerves, is removed. Advances in options have produced effective alternatives to traditional Discectomy procedures (i.e. MicroDiscectomy, Endoscopic Discectomy, and Laser Discectomy). A laminectomy is often involved to permit access to the intervertebral disc in a traditional Discectomy.
Electroencephalography	Electroencephalography (EEG) is the recording of electrical activity along the scalp produced by the firing of neurons within the brain. In clinical contexts, EEG refers to the recording of the brain's spontaneous electrical activity over a short period of time, usually 20-40 minutes, as recorded from multiple electrodes placed on the scalp. In neurology, the main diagnostic application of EEG is in the case of epilepsy, as epileptic activity can create clear abnormalities on a standard EEG study.
Nerve	A Nerve is an enclosed, cable-like bundle of peripheral axons (the long, slender projections of neurons). A Nerve provides a common pathway for the electrochemical Nerve impulses that are transmitted along each of the axons. Nerves are found only in the peripheral nervous system.
Skull	The skull is a bony structure found in the head of many animals. The skull supports the structures of the face and protects the head against injury. The skull can be divided into two parts: the cranium and the mandible.

Chapter 3. PART III: Chapter 9 - Chapter 13

Vertebral column	In human anatomy, the Vertebral column is a column usually consisting of 33 vertebrae, the sacrum, intervertebral discs, and the coccyx situated in the dorsal aspect of the torso, separated by spinal discs. It houses and protects the spinal cord in its spinal canal. Viewed laterally the Vertebral column presents several curves, which correspond to the different regions of the column, and are called cervical, thoracic, lumbar, and pelvic.
Deltoideus	In human anatomy, the deltoid muscle is the muscle forming the rounded contour of the shoulder. Anatomically, it appears to be made up of three distinct sets of fibers though electromyography suggests that it consists of at least seven groups that can be independently coordinated by the central nervous system. It was previously called the Deltoideus and the name is still used by some anatomists.
Dementia	Dementia (meaning `deprived of mind`) is a serious cognitive disorder. It may be static, the result of a unique global brain injury or progressive, resulting in long-term decline in cognitive function due to damage or disease in the body beyond what might be expected from normal aging. Although Dementia is far more common in the geriatric population, it may occur in any stage of adulthood.
Vascular	Vascular in zoology and medicine means `related to blood vessels`, which are part of the circulatory system. An organ or tissue that is Vascularized is heavily endowed with blood vessels and thus richly supplied with blood. In botany, plants with a dedicated transport system for water and nutrients are called Vascular plants.
Amyotrophic lateral sclerosis	Amyotrophic lateral sclerosis is a form of motor neuron disease. Amyotrophic lateral sclerosis is a progressive, fatal, neurodegenerative disease caused by the degeneration of motor neurons, the nerve cells in the central nervous system that control voluntary muscle movement. The condition is often called Lou Gehrig's Disease in North America, after the famous New York Yankees baseball player who was diagnosed with the disease in 1939 and died from it in 1941, at age thirty-seven.
Degenerative disease	A Degenerative disease is a disease in which the function or structure of the affected tissues or organs will progressively deteriorate over time, whether due to normal bodily wear or lifestyle choices such as exercise or eating habits. Degenerative diseases are often contrasted with infectious diseases.

· Amyotrophic Lateral Sclerosis (ALS), e.g., Lou Gehrig`s Disease

· Parkinson`s Disease

· Multiple system atrophy

· Niemann Pick disease

· Atherosclerosis

· Progressive supranuclear palsy

· Cancer

· Tay-Sachs Disease

· Diabetes

· Heart Disease

· Inflammatory Bowel Disease (IBD)

· Prostatitis

· Osteoarthritis

· Osteoporosis

· Rheumatoid Arthritis .

| Sclerosis | Sclerosis or sclerotization is a hardening of tissue and other anatomical features;

· Sclerosis

· Cyberbrain Sclerosis, a fictional disease introduced in Ghost in the Shell: Stand Alone Complex. The disease is characterized by hardening of the brain tissues precipitated by the cyberization process. |

	· a process which hardens plant tissue by adding fibers and sclereids, resulting in sclerenchyma
Multiple sclerosis	Multiple sclerosis is a disease in which the fatty myelin sheaths around the axons of the brain and spinal cord are damaged, leading to demyelination and scarring as well as a broad spectrum of signs and symptoms. Disease onset usually occurs in young adults, and it is more common in females. It has a prevalence that ranges between 2 and 150 per 100,000. Multiple sclerosis was first described in 1868 by Jean-Martin Charcot.
Myasthenia gravis	Myasthenia gravis is a neuromuscular disease leading to fluctuating muscle weakness and fatiguability. It is an autoimmune disorder, in which weakness is caused by circulating antibodies that block acetylcholine receptors at the post-synaptic neuromuscular junction, inhibiting the stimulative effect of the neurotransmitter acetylcholine. Myasthenia is treated medically with cholinesterase inhibitors or immunosuppressants, and, in selected cases, thymectomy.
Gravis	Gravis can have multiple meanings: · Gramin Vikas Vigyan Samiti, an Indian NGO · Advanced Gravis Computer Technology, manufacturer of computer peripherals and joysticks
Poliomyelitis	Poliomyelitis, often called polio or infantile paralysis, is an acute viral infectious disease spread from person to person, primarily via the fecal-oral route. The term derives from the Greek poliós , meaning `grey`, myelós (ÂμυελΐŒς), referring to the `spinal cord`, and the suffix -itis, which denotes inflammation. Although around 90% of polio infections cause no symptoms at all, affected individuals can exhibit a range of symptoms if the virus enters the blood stream.
Hydrocephalus	Hydrocephalus , also known as Water on the Brain, is a medical condition. People with Hydrocephalus have an abnormal accumulation of cerebrospinal fluid in the ventricles, or cavities, of the brain. This may cause increased intracranial pressure inside the skull and progressive enlargement of the head, convulsion, and mental disability.

Chapter 3. PART III: Chapter 9 - Chapter 13

Mental disorder	A Mental disorder or mental illness is a psychological or behavioral pattern that occurs in an individual and is thought to cause distress or disability that is not expected as part of normal development or culture. The recognition and understanding of Mental disorders has changed over time and across cultures. Definitions, assessments, and classifications of Mental disorders can vary, but guideline criteria listed in the ICD, DSM and other manuals are widely accepted by mental health professionals.
Spina bifida	Spina bifida is a developmental birth defect caused by the incomplete closure of the embryonic neural tube. Some vertebrae overlying the spinal cord are not fully formed and remain unfused and open. If the opening is large enough, this allows a portion of the spinal cord to stick out through the opening in the bones.
Depression	Depression is a term that can refer to a wide variety of abnormal variations in an individual's mood. If changes in an individual's mood are persistent and cause distress or impairment in functioning, then a mood disorder may be present. Individuals with mood disorders experience extremes of emotions, for example sadness, that are higher in intensity and longer in duration than normal.
Transient ischemic attack	A transient ischemic attack is a change in the blood supply to a particular area of the brain, resulting in brief neurologic dysfunction that persists, by definition, for less than 24 hours. If symptoms persist longer, then it is categorized as a stroke. A cerebral infarct that lasts longer than 24 hours, but less than 72 hours is termed a reversible ischemic neurologic deficit or RIND. Symptoms vary widely from person to person, depending on the area of the brain involved.
Stroke	A stroke is the rapidly developing loss of brain function(s) due to disturbance in the blood supply to the brain. This can be due to ischemia (lack of glucose ' oxygen supply) caused by thrombosis or embolism or due to a hemorrhage. As a result, the affected area of the brain is unable to function, leading to inability to move one or more limbs on one side of the body, inability to understand or The traditional definition of stroke, devised by the World Health Organization in the 1970s, is a 'neurological deficit of cerebrovascular cause that persists beyond 24 hours or is interrupted by death within 24 hours'.
Encephalitis	Encephalitis is an acute inflammation of the brain.

301

	Encephalitis with meningitis is known as meningoEncephalitis.
	Encephalitis.
Absence seizures	Absence seizures are one of several kinds of seizures. These seizures are sometimes referred to as petit mal seizures . In Absence seizures, the person may appear to be staring into space with or without jerking or twitching movements of the eye muscles.
Brain abscess	Brain abscess is an abscess caused by inflammation and collection of infected material, coming from local (ear infection, dental abscess, infection of paranasal sinuses, infection of the mastoid air cells of the temporal bone, epidural abscess) or remote (lung, heart, kidney etc). infectious sources, within the brain tissue. The infection may also be introduced through a skull fracture following a head trauma or surgical procedures.
Epilepsy	Epilepsy is a common chronic neurological disorder characterized by recurrent unprovoked seizures. These seizures are transient signs and/or symptoms of abnormal, excessive or synchronous neuronal activity in the brain. About 50 million people worldwide have Epilepsy, with almost 90% of these people being in developing countries.
Seizure	An epileptic Seizure, occasionally referred to as a fit, is defined as a transient symptom of `abnormal excessive or synchronous neuronal activity in the brain`. The outward effect can be as dramatic as a wild thrashing movement (tonic-clonic Seizure) or as mild as a brief loss of awareness. It can manifest as an alteration in mental state, tonic or clonic movements, convulsions, and various other psychic symptoms (such as déjà vu or jamais vu).
Abscess	An Abscess is a collection of pus that has accumulated in a cavity formed by the tissue on the basis of an infectious process (usually caused by bacteria or parasites) or other foreign materials (e.g. splinters, bullet wounds, or injecting needles). It is a defensive reaction of the tissue to prevent the spread of infectious materials to other parts of the body. The organisms or foreign materials kill the local cells, resulting in the release of cytokines.
Seizure	An epileptic Seizure, occasionally referred to as a fit, is defined as a transient symptom of `abnormal excessive or synchronous neuronal activity in the brain`. The outward effect can be as dramatic as a wild thrashing movement (tonic-clonic Seizure) or as mild as a brief loss of awareness. It can manifest as an alteration in mental state, tonic or clonic movements, convulsions, and various other psychic symptoms (such as déjà vu or jamais vu).

Concussion	Concussion, from the Latin concutera or the Latin concussus (`action of striking together`), is the most common type of traumatic brain injury. The terms mild brain injury, mild traumatic brain injury (MTBI), mild head injury (MHI), and minor head trauma and Concussion may be used interchangeably, although the latter is often treated as a narrower category. The term `Concussion` has been used for centuries and is still commonly used in sports medicine, while `MTBI` is a technical term used more commonly nowadays in general medical contexts.
Hematoma	A Hematoma, or haematoma, is a collection of blood outside the blood vessels, generally the result of hemorrhage, or more specifically, internal bleeding. It is commonly called a bruise.
Hepatitis	Hepatitis (plural hepatitides) implies injury to the liver characterized by the presence of inflammatory cells in the tissue of the organ. The name is from ancient Greek hepar , the root being hepat- (á¼¡πατ-), meaning liver, and suffix -itis, meaning `inflammation` (c. 1727).
Hepatitis D	Hepatitis D, also referred to as Hepatitis D virus (HDV) and classified as Hepatitis Delta virus, is a disease caused by a small circular RNA virus. HDV is considered to be a subviral satellite because it can propagate only in the presence of the Hepatitis B virus (HBV). Transmission of HDV can occur either via simultaneous infection with HBV (coinfection) or via infection of an individual previously infected with HBV (superinfection).
Traumatic brain injury	Traumatic brain injury occurs when an external force traumatically injures the brain. Traumatic brain injury can be classified based on severity, mechanism , or other features (e.g. occurring in a specific location or over a widespread area). Head injury usually refers to Traumatic brain injury, but is a broader category because it can involve damage to structures other than the brain, such as the scalp and skull.
Angiomas	Angiomas are benign tumors that are made up of small blood vessels or lymph vessels.
Astrocytoma	Astrocytomas are cancers of the brain that originate in star-shaped brain cells called astrocytes. They account for roughly 75% of neuroepithelial tumors.
	Of numerous grading systems in use, the most common is the World Health Organization (WHO) grading system for Astrocytoma.
Eosinophilia	Eosinophilia is the state of having a high concentration of eosinophils (eosinophil granulocytes) in the blood. The normal concentration is between 0 and 0.5×10^9 eosinophils per litre of blood. Eosinophilia can be reactive (in response to other stimuli such as allergy or infection) or non reactive.

Ependymoma	Ependymoma is a tumor that arises from the ependyma, a tissue of the central nervous system. Usually, in children the location is intracranial, while in adults it is spinal. The common location of intracranial Ependymoma is the fourth ventricle.
Germ cells	In biology, Germ cells are the cells that give rise to the gametes of organisms that reproduce sexually. In many animals, the Germ cells originate near the gut and migrate to the developing gonads. There, they undergo cell division of two types, mitosis and meiosis, followed by cellular differentiation into mature gametes, either eggs or sperm.
Glioma	A Glioma is a type of tumor that starts in the brain or spine. It is called a Glioma because it arises from glial cells. The most common site of Gliomas is the brain.
Hemangioblastoma	Hemangioblastoma of the central nervous system is a benign tumor (WHO grade I) that is typically cystic and can occur throughout the central nervous system. It is a tumor composed of hemangioblasts, a type of stem cell that normally give rise to blood vessels or blood cells. Its name breaks down to Greek roots as follows: Haema , angeion (vessel), blastos (embryonic), oma (tumor).
Oligodendrocytes	Oligodendrocytes , or oligodendroglia , are a type of brain cell. They are a variety of neuroglia (specifically, a sub-type of macroglia). Their main function is the insulation of axons (the long projection of nerve cells) in the central nervous system (the brain and spinal cord) of higher vertebrates.
Reflux	Reflux is a technique involving the condensation of vapors and the return of this condensate to the system from which it originated. It is used in industrial and laboratory distillations. It is also used in chemistry to supply energy to reactions over a long period of time.
Tumor	A tumor or tumour is the name for a swelling or lesion formed by an abnormal growth of cells (termed neoplastic). tumor is not synonymous with cancer. A tumor can be benign, pre-malignant or malignant, whereas cancer is by definition malignant.
Medulloblastoma	Medulloblastoma is a highly malignant primary brain tumor that originates in the cerebellum or posterior fossa. Originally considered to be a glioma, Medulloblastoma is now known to be of the family of cranial primitive neuroectodermal tumors (PNET). Tumors that originate in the cerebellum are referred to as infratentorial because they occur below the tentorium, a thick membrane that separates the cerebral hemispheres of the brain from the cerebellum.

Meningiomas	Meningiomas are the second most common primary tumor of the central nervous system, arising from the arachnoid `cap` cells of the arachnoid villi in the meninges. These tumors are usually benign in nature; however, they can be malignant. Most cases are sporadic while some are familial.
Pituitary tumors	Pituitary adenomas are tumors that occur in the pituitary gland, and account for about 10% of intracranial neoplasms. They often remain undiagnosed, and small pituitary tumors have an estimated prevalence of 16.7% (14.4% in autopsy studies and 22.5% in radiologic studies). pituitary tumors were, historically, classed as basophilic, acidophilic, or chromophobic on the basis of whether or not they took up the stains hematoxylin and eosin.
Muscle	Muscle is the contractile tissue of animals and is derived from the mesodermal layer of embryonic germ cells. Muscle cells contain contractile filaments that move past each other and change the size of the cell. They are classified as skeletal, cardiac, or smooth Muscles.
Cornea	The Cornea is the transparent front part of the eye that covers the iris, pupil, and anterior chamber. Together with the lens, the Cornea refracts light, accounting for approximately two-thirds of the eye's total optical power. In humans, the refractive power of the Cornea is approximately 43 dioptres.
Sclera	The Sclera, also known as the white part of the eye, is the opaque (usually white, though certain animals, such as horses and lizards, can have black Sclera), fibrous, protective, outer layer of the eye containing collagen and elastic fiber. In the development of the embryo, the Sclera is derived from the neural crest. In children, it is thinner and shows some of the underlying pigment, appearing slightly blue.
Choroid	The Choroid, also known as the Choroidea or Choroid coat, is the vascular layer containing connective tissue, of the eye lying between the retina and the sclera. In humans its thickness is about 0.5 mm. The Choroid provides oxygen and nourishment to the outer layers of the retina .
Conjunctiva	The Conjunctiva is a clear mucous membrane consisting of cells and underlying basement membrane that covers the sclera (white part of the eye) and lines the inside of the eyelids. It is made up of the rare non-keratinizing squamous epithelium.
Lens	Lens can refer to:

· Lens an optical element which converges or diverges light

· Lens a part of the eye

· Corrective Lens for correction of human vision

· Contact Lens, placed on the cornea of the eye

· Photographic Lens, a Lens designed for use on a camera.

Retina	The vertebrate Retina is a light sensitive tissue lining the inner surface of the eye. The optics of the eye create an image of the visual world on the Retina, which serves much the same function as the film in a camera. Light striking the Retina initiates a cascade of chemical and electrical events that ultimately trigger nerve impulses.
Taste	Taste is a form of direct chemoreception and is one of the traditional five senses. It refers to the ability to detect the flavor of substances such as food, certain minerals, and poisons. In humans and many other vertebrate animals the sense of Taste partners with the less direct sense of smell, in the brain's perception of flavor.
Astigmatism	An optical system with Astigmatism is one where rays that propagate in two perpendicular planes have different foci. If an optical system with Astigmatism is used to form an image of a cross, the vertical and horizontal lines will be in sharp focus at two different distances. The term comes from the Greek α- meaning 'without' and στῖγμα (stigma), 'a mark, spot, puncture'.
Blepharitis	Blepharitis is an ocular disease characterized by inflammation of the eyelid margins. Blepharitis may cause redness of the eyes, itching and irritation of the eyelids in one or both eyes. Its appearance is often confused with conjunctivitis and due to its recurring nature it is the most common cause of 'recurrent conjunctivitis' in older people.
Cataract	A Cataract is a clouding that develops in the crystalline lens of the eye or in its envelope, varying in degree from slight to complete opacity and obstructing the passage of light. Early in the development of age-related Cataract the power of the lens may be increased, causing near-sightedness (myopia), and the gradual yellowing and opacification of the lens may reduce the perception of blue colours. Cataracts typically progress slowly to cause vision loss and are potentially blinding if untreated.

Chapter 3. PART III: Chapter 9 - Chapter 13

Chalazion	A Chalazion pronounced is a cyst in the eyelid that is caused by inflammation of a blocked meibomian gland, usually on the upper eyelid. Chalazions differ from styes (hordeolums) in that they are less painful than styes, but bigger in size (chalazia tend to be larger than styes). A Chalazion or meibomian cyst could take months to fully heal with treatment and could take years to heal without any.
Cholesteatoma	Cholesteatoma is a destructive and expanding keratinizing squamous epithelium in the middle ear and/or mastoid process. There are two types: congenital and acquired. Acquired Cholesteatomas can be caused by a tear or retraction of the ear drum.
Dacryocystitis	Dacryocystitis is an infection of the nasolacrimal sac, frequently caused by nasolacrimal duct obstruction. The term derives from the Greek dákryon , cyst (sac), and -itis (inflammation). It causes pain, redness, and swelling over the inner aspect of the lower eyelid and epiphora.
Ectropion	Ectropion is a medical condition in which the lower eyelid turns outwards. It is one of the notable aspects of newborns exhibiting Harlequin type ichthyosis. The condition can be repaired surgically.
Entropion	Entropion is a medical condition in which the eyelids fold inward. It is very uncomfortable, as the eyelashes rub against the cornea constantly. Entropion is usually caused by genetic factors and may be congenital.
Enucleation	Enucleation is removal of the eye, leaving the eye muscles and remaining orbital contents intact. This type of ocular surgery is indicated for a number of different ocular tumors, in eyes that have suffered severe trauma, and in eyes that are blind and painful due to other disease. Auto-Enucleation (oedipism) and other forms of serious self inflicted eye injury are an extremely rare form of severe self-harm which usually results from serious mental illnesses such as schizophrenia .
Examination	A competitive Examination is an Examination where applicants compete for a limited number of positions, as opposed to merely having to reach a certain level to pass. A comprehensive Examination is a specific type of exam taken by graduate students, which may determine their eligibility to continue their studies.

	In the UK an Examination is usually supervised by an invigilator.
Exophthalmos	Exophthalmos is a bulging of the eye anteriorly out of the orbit. Exophthalmos can be either bilateral or unilateral . Measurement of the degree of Exophthalmos is performed using an exophthalmometer.
Exostosis	An Exostosis is the formation of new bone on the surface of a bone. Exostosis can cause chronic pain ranging from mild to debilitatingly severe, depending on where they are located and what shape they are. The overgrowth of outer ear canal bone is the body's way of protecting the ear drum from the frequent rush of cold water against it which commonly occurs with surfing.
Fenestration	The word Fenestration finds its root in the Latin word for window, fenestra. Architecture · Products that fill openings in a building envelope, such as windows, doors, skylights, curtain walls, etc., designed to permit the passage of air, light, vehicles, or people.
Glaucoma	Glaucoma refers to a group of diseases that affect the optic nerve and involves a loss of retinal ganglion cells in a characteristic pattern. It is a type of optic neuropathy. Raised intraocular pressure is a significant risk factor for developing Glaucoma (above 22 mmHg or 2.9 kPa).
Hyperopia	Hyperopia, also known as farsightedness, longsightedness or hypermetropia, is a defect of vision caused by an imperfection in the eye (often when the eyeball is too short or when the lens cannot become round enough), causing difficulty focusing on near objects, and in extreme cases causing a sufferer to be unable to focus on objects at any distance. As an object moves toward the eye, the eye must increase its power to keep the image in focus on the retina. If the power of the cornea and lens is insufficient, as in Hyperopia, the image will appear blurred.
Keratomalacia	Keratomalacia is an eye disorder that leads to a dry cornea. One of its major causes is Vitamin A deficiency.
Atresia	Atresia is a condition in which a body orifice or passage in the body is abnormally closed or absent.

Examples of Atresia include:

· Anorectal Atresia - malformation of the opening between the rectum and anus.

· Aural (External Auditory Canal) Atresia- Absence of the ear canal or failure of the canal to be tubular or fully formed (can be related to Microtia- a congenital deformity of the pinna (outer ear)).

Labyrinth	In Greek mythology, the Labyrinth was an elaborate structure designed and built by the legendary artificer Daedalus for King Minos of Crete at Knossos. Its function was to hold the Minotaur, a creature that was half man and half bull and was eventually killed by the Athenian hero Theseus. Daedalus had made the Labyrinth so cunningly that he himself could barely escape it after he built it.
Labyrinthitis	Labyrinthitis is an inflammation of the inner ear. It derives its name from the labyrinths that house the vestibular system (which sense changes in head position). Labyrinthitis can cause balance disorders.
Myometrium	The Myometrium is the middle layer of the uterine wall consisting of smooth muscle cells and supporting stromal and vascular tissue. The inner layer of the uterine wall is the endometrium or uterine lining, and the outer layer the serosa or perimetrium. The Myometrium stretches (the smooth muscle cells expand in both size and number) during pregnancy to allow for the harboring of the pregnancy, and contracts in a coordinated fashion during the process of labor.
Myringotomy	Myringotomy is a surgical procedure in which a tiny incision is created in the eardrum, so as to relieve pressure caused by the excessive build-up of fluid, or to drain pus. Myringotomy is often performed as a treatment for otitis media. If a patient requires Myringotomy for drainage or ventilation of the middle ear, this generally implies that the Eustachian tube is either partially or completely obstructed and is not able to perform this function in its usual physiologic fashion.

Ophthalmoscopy	Ophthalmoscopy is a test that allows a health professional to see inside the fundus of the eye and other structures using an ophthalmoscope. It is done as part of an eye examination and may be done as part of a routine physical examination. The invention of the ophthalmoscope in 1850 by Hermann Von Helmholtz revoulutionized ophthalmology.
	It is of two major types:
	· Direct Ophthalmoscopy
	· Indirect Ophthalmoscopy
	· Slit-lamp Ophthalmoscopy Ophthalmoscopy is done as part of a routine physical or complete eye examination.
Otitis	Otitis is a general term for inflammation or infection of the ear, in both humans and other animals.
	It is subdivided into the following:
	· Otitis externa, external Otitis, or `swimmer`s ear` involves the outer ear and ear canal. In external Otitis, the ear hurts when touched or pulled.
	· Otitis media or middle ear infection involves the middle ear. In Otitis media, the ear is infected or clogged with fluid behind the ear drum, in the normally air-filled middle-ear space.
Otitis media	Otitis media is inflammation of the middle ear, or middle ear infection .

	Otitis media occurs in the area between the ear drum and the inner ear, including a duct known as the Eustachian tube. It is one of the two categories of ear inflammation that can underlie what is commonly called an earache, the other being otitis externa.
Papilledema	Papilledema is optic disc swelling that is caused by increased intracranial pressure. The swelling is usually bilateral but can be unilateral which is extremely rare and can occur over a period of hours to weeks.
	In intracranial hypertension Papilledema can occur in only one eye or it can be more severe in one eye than the other or may not occur at all despite evidence of raised intracranial hypertension.
Pathology	Pathology is the study and diagnosis of disease through examination of organs, tissues, bodily fluids, and whole bodies (autopsies). The term also encompasses the related scientific study of disease processes, called General Pathology. Medical Pathology is divided in two main branches, Anatomical Pathology and Clinical Pathology.
Popliteal	Popliteal refers to anatomical structures located in the back of the knee: · Popliteal artery · Popliteal vein · Popliteal fossa · Popliteal lymph nodes · Popliteal nerves · Popliteal pterygium
Ptosis	Ptosis (πτωσις `falling, a fall`) refers to droopiness of any body part. Specifically, it can refer to: · Ptosis (eyelid)

· Ptosis (breasts)

· NephroPtosis (kidney)

· GastroPtosis (stomach) .

Strabismus	Strabismus is a condition in which the eyes are not properly aligned with each other. It typically involves a lack of coordination between the extraocular muscles that prevents bringing the gaze of each eye to the same point in space and preventing proper binocular vision, which may adversely affect depth perception. Strabismus can be either a disorder of the brain in coordinating the eyes, or of one or more of the relevant muscles` power or direction of motion.
Tarsorrhaphy	Tarsorrhaphy is a surgical procedure in which the eyelids are partially sewn together to narrow the opening (i.e. palpebral fissure). .
Tinnitus	Tinnitus is the perception of sound within the human ear in the absence of corresponding external sound. Tinnitus is not a disease but a symptom resulting from a range of underlying causes that can include ear infections, foreign objects or wax in the ear, nose allergies that prevent (or induce) fluid drain and cause wax build-up. Tinnitus can also be caused by natural hearing impairment (as in aging), as a side-effect of some medications, and as a side-effect of genetic (congenital) hearing loss.
Tympanometry	Tympanometry is an examination used to test the condition of the middle ear and mobility of the eardrum (tympanic membrane) and the conduction bones by creating variations of air pressure in the ear canal. Tympanometry is an objective test of middle-ear function. It is not a hearing test, but rather a measure of energy transmission through the middle ear.

Chapter 3. PART III: Chapter 9 - Chapter 13

Chapter 3. PART III: Chapter 9 - Chapter 13

Infection	An Infection is the detrimental colonization of a host organism by a foreign species. In an Infection, the infecting organism seeks to utilize the host's resources to multiply, usually at the expense of the host. The infecting organism, or pathogen, interferes with the normal functioning of the host and can lead to chronic wounds, gangrene, loss of an infected limb, and even death.
Amblyopia	Amblyopia, otherwise known as lazy eye, is a disorder of the visual system that is characterized by poor or indistinct vision in an eye that is otherwise physically normal, or out of proportion to associated structural abnormalities. It has been estimated to affect 1-5% of the population. The problem is caused by either no transmission or poor transmission of the visual image to the brain for a sustained period of dysfunction or during early childhood.
Diplopia	Diplopia, commonly known as double vision, is the simultaneous perception of two images of a single object. These images may be displaced horizontally, vertically, or diagonally (i.e. both vertically and horizontally) in relation to each other. Binocular Diplopia is double vision arising as a result of the misalignment of the two eyes relative to each other, such as occurs in esotropia or exotropia.
Presbyopia	Presbyopia describes the condition where the eye exhibits a progressively diminished ability to focus on near objects with age. Presbyopia's exact mechanisms are not known with certainty; however, the research evidence most strongly supports a loss of elasticity of the crystalline lens, although changes in the lens's curvature from continual growth and loss of power of the ciliary muscles (the muscles that bend and straighten the lens) have also been postulated as its cause. Similar to grey hair and wrinkles, Presbyopia is a symptom caused by the natural course of aging; the direct translation of the condition's name is 'elder eye'.
Conjunctivitis	Conjunctivitis (commonly called 'pink eye' or 'Madras eye') is an inflammation of the conjunctiva (the outermost layer of the eye and the inner surface of the eyelids), most commonly due to an allergic reaction or an infection (usually viral, but sometimes bacterial BlepharoConjunctivitis is the dual combination of Conjunctivitis with blepharitis (inflammation of the eyelids).
Descending colon	The Descending colon of humans passes downward through the left hypochondrium and lumbar regions, along the lateral border of the left kidney.

	At the lower end of the kidney it turns medialward toward the lateral border of the psoas muscle, and then descends, in the angle between psoas and quadratus lumborum, to the crest of the ilium, where it ends in the sigmoid colon.
	The peritoneum covers its anterior surface and sides, and therefore the Descending colon is described as retroperitoneal.
Colon	The colon is the last part of the digestive system in most vertebrates; it extracts water and salt from solid wastes before they are eliminated from the body, and is the site in which flora-aided (largely bacteria) fermentation of unabsorbed material occurs. Unlike the small intestine, the colon does not play a major role in absorption of foods and nutrients. However, the colon does absorb water, potassium and some fat soluble vitamins.
Glans penis	The Glans penis is the sensitive bulbous structure at the distal end of the penis. It is also commonly referred to as the `head` of the penis. Slang terms include `helmet`, `nob` (or `knob`), and `bell end`, and all refer to its distinctive shape.
Penis	The Penis (plural Penises, penes) is an external sexual organ of certain biologically male organisms, in both vertebrates and invertebrates. The Penis is a reproductive organ, technically an intromittent organ, and for placental mammals, additionally serves as the external organ of urination. The Penis is generally found on mammals and reptiles.
Conductive hearing loss	Conductive hearing loss happens when there is a problem conducting sound waves through the outer ear, tympanic membrane (eardrum) or middle ear (ossicles). This type of hearing loss may occur in conjunction with sensorineural hearing loss or alone. · Cerumen (earwax) · Otitis externa · Foreign body in the external auditory canal (not always) · Exostoses

· Tumour of the ear canal

· Congenital atresia

· Acute otitis media

· Serous otitis media

· Tympanic membrane perforation

· Cholesteatoma

· Otosclerosis

· Middle ear tumour

· Temporal bone trauma

Severe Otosclerosis, form of mechanical Conductive hearing loss most commonly found in people who have been subjected to intense noise. Occurs when there is an obstruction in either the oval window and/or the round window.

Otitis externa	Otitis externa (`swimmer`s ear`) is an inflammation of the outer ear and ear canal. Along with otitis media, external otitis is one of the two human conditions commonly called `earache`. It also occurs in many other species.
Coccyx	The Coccyx , commonly referred to as the tailbone, is the final segment of the human vertebral column. Comprising three to five separate or fused vertebrae below the sacrum, it is attached to the sacrum by a fibrocartilaginous joint, the sacrococcygeal symphysis, which permits limited movement between the sacrum and the Coccyx.

	The term Coccyx comes originally from the Greek language and means `cuckoo`, referring to the curved shape of a cuckoo`s beak when viewed from the side.
Cochlea	The Cochlea is the auditory portion of the inner ear. Its core component is the Organ of Corti, the sensory organ of hearing, which is distributed along the partition separating fluid chambers in the coiled tapered tube of the Cochlea. The name is from the Latin for snail, which is from the Greek kokhlias , from kokhlos (`spiral shell`) (etymology), in reference to its coiled shape; the Cochlea is coiled in most mammals, monotremes being the exceptions.
Idiopathic	Idiopathic is an adjective used primarily in medicine meaning arising spontaneously or from an obscure or unknown cause. From Greek á¼´διος, idios + πÎ¬θος, pathos (suffering), it means approximately `a disease of its own kind.` It is technically a term from nosology, the classification of disease. For most medical conditions, one or more causes are somewhat understood, but in a certain percentage of people with the condition, the cause may not be readily apparent or characterized.
Retinal	Retinal is one of the many forms of vitamin A . Retinal is a polyene chromophore, and bound to proteins called opsins, is the chemical basis of animal vision. Bound to proteins called type 1 rhodopsins, Retinal allows certain microorganisms to convert light into metabolic energy.
Blood	Blood is a specialized bodily fluid that delivers necessary substances to the body's cells -- such as nutrients and oxygen -- and transports waste products away from those same cells. In vertebrates, it is composed of Blood cells suspended in a liquid called Blood plasma. Plasma, which comprises 55% of Blood fluid, is mostly water (90% by volume), and contains dissolved proteins, glucose, mineral ions, hormones, carbon dioxide (plasma being the main medium for excretory product transportation), platelets and Blood cells themselves.
Medicare fraud	In the United States, Medicare fraud is a general term that refers to an individual or corporation that seeks to collect Medicare health care reimbursement under false pretenses. There are many different types of Medicare fraud, all of which have the same goal: to bilk money from the Medicare program. The general scam is believed to have started in South Florida; specifically, Miami-Dade.

Chapter 3. PART III: Chapter 9 - Chapter 13

Abuse	Abuse is defined as: Abuse of information typically involves a breach of confidence or plagiarism. Abuse of power, in the form of 'malfeasance in office' or 'official misconduct', is the commission of an unlawful act, done in an official capacity, which affects the performance of official duties. Malfeasance in office is often grounds for a for cause removal of an elected official by statute or recall election.
Health care	Health care , refers to the treatment and management of illness, and the preservation of health through services offered by the medical, dental, complementary and alternative medicine, pharmaceutical, clinical laboratory sciences , nursing, and allied health professions. Health care embraces all the goods and services designed to promote health, including `preventive, curative and palliative interventions, whether directed to individuals or to populations`. Before the term Health care became popular, English-speakers referred to medicine or to the health sector and spoke of the treatment and prevention of illness and disease.
Attending physician	In the United States, an Attending physician is a physician who has completed residency and practices medicine in a clinic or hospital, in the speciality learned during residency. An Attending physician can supervise fellows, residents and medical students. Attending physicians may also have an academic title at an affiliated university such as 'professor'.
Clavicle	In human anatomy, the Clavicle or collar bone is classified as a long bone that makes up part of the shoulder girdle (pectoral girdle). It receives its name from the Latin clavicula because the bone rotates along its axis like a key when the shoulder is abducted. This movement is palpable.
Managed care	The term Managed care is used to describe a variety of techniques intended to reduce the cost of providing health benefits and improve the quality of care (`Managed care techniques`) f), or to describe systems of financing and delivering health care to enrollees organized around Managed care techniques and concepts (`Managed care delivery systems`). According to the United States National Library of Medicine, the term `Managed care` encompasses programs:

...intended to reduce unnecessary health care costs through a variety of mechanisms, including: economic incentives for physicians and patients to select less costly forms of care; programs for reviewing the medical necessity of specific services; increased beneficiary cost sharing; controls on inpatient admissions and lengths of stay; the establishment of cost-sharing incentives for outpatient surgery; selective contracting with health care providers; and the intensive management of high-cost health care cases. The programs may be provided in a variety of settings, such as Health Maintenance Organizations and Preferred Provider Organizations.

Nurse anesthetist	A Nurse anesthetist is a registered nurse and advanced practice nurse who has acquired additional education to administer anesthesia. In the United States, education is overseen by the American Association of Nurse anesthetists AANurse anesthetist Council on Accreditation of Nurse Anesthesia Educational Programs. The Nurse anesthetist's education and official title vary in different nations.
Preferred Provider Organization	In health insurance in the United States, a Preferred Provider Organization is a managed care organization of medical doctors, hospitals, and other health care providers who have covenanted with an insurer or a third-party administrator to provide health care at reduced rates to the insurer's or administrator's clients. A Preferred Provider Organization is a subscription-based medical care arrangement. A membership allows a substantial discount below their regularly charged rates from the designated professionals partnered with the organization.
Physician	A Physician -- also known as medical practitioner, doctor of medicine, medical doctor which is concerned with maintaining or restoring human health through the study, diagnosis, and treatment of disease or injury. This properly requires both a detailed knowledge of the academic disciplines underlying diseases and their treatment -- the science of medicine -- and also a decent competence in its applied practice -- the art or craft of medicine. Both the role of the Physician and the meaning of the word itself vary significantly around the world, but as generally understood, the ethics of medicine require that Physicians show consideration, compassion and benevolence for their patients.
Terminology	Terminology therefore denotes a more formal discipline which systematically studies the labelling or designating of concepts particular to one or more subject fields or domains of human activity, through research and analysis of terms in context, for the purpose of documenting and promoting correct usage. This study can be limited to one language or can cover more than one language at the same time (multilingual Terminology, bilingual Terminology, and so forth) or may focus on studies of terms across fields.

	Terminology is not connected to information retrieval in any way but focused on the meaning and conveyance of concepts.
Deductible	In an insurance policy, the Deductible (North American term) or excess (UK term) is the portion of any claim that is not covered by the insurance provider. It is the amount of expenses that must be paid out of pocket before an insurer will cover any expenses. It is normally quoted as a fixed quantity and is a part of most policies covering losses to the policy holder.
Durable medical equipment	Durable medical equipment is a term of art used to describe any medical equipment used in the home to aid in a better quality of living. It is a benefit included in most Insurances. In some cases certain Medicare benefits, that is, whether Medicare may pay for the item.
Explanation of Benefits	An Explanation of Benefits is a statement sent to covered individuals explaining what medical treatment and/or services were paid for on their behalf.
	On August 28, 2007 Judge David W. O`Brien announced, with significant input from the California Dept of Insurance, District Attorneys and the Employers` Fraud Task Force, The O`Brien Form. Medicare has for years sent an Explanation of Benefits to beneficiaries advising them of payments made to medical providers on the beneficiaries behalf.
Medical record	A Medical record, health record, or medical chart is a systematic documentation of a patient`s medical history and care. The term `Medical record` is used both for the physical folder for each individual patient and for the body of information which comprises the total of each patient`s health history. Medical records are intensely personal documents and there are many ethical and legal issues surrounding them such as the degree of third-party access and appropriate storage and disposal.
Medical equipment	Medical equipment is designed to aid in the diagnosis, monitoring or treatment of medical conditions. These devices are usually designed with rigorous safety standards. There are several basic types:
	· Diagnostic equipment includes medical imaging machines, used to aid in diagnosis.

Chapter 3. PART III: Chapter 9 - Chapter 13

Authorization	Authorization is the function of specifying access rights to resources, which is related to information security and computer security in general and to access control in particular. More formally, 'to authorize' is to define access policy. For example, human resources staff are normally authorized to access employee records, and this policy is usually formalized as access control rules in a computer system.
Respiratory tract	In humans the Respiratory tract is the part of the anatomy that has to do with the process of respiration. The Respiratory tract is divided into 3 segments: · Upper Respiratory tract: nose and nasal passages, paranasal sinuses, and throat or pharynx · Respiratory airways: voice box or larynx, trachea, bronchi, and bronchioles · Lungs: respiratory bronchioles, alveolar ducts, alveolar sacs, and alveoli The Respiratory tract is a common site for infections. Upper Respiratory tract infections are probably the most common infections in the world. Most of the Respiratory tract exists merely as a piping system for air to travel in the lungs; alveoli are the only part of the lung that exchanges oxygen and carbon dioxide with the blood.
Radiology	Radiology is the branch or speciality of medicine that deals with the study and application of imaging technology like x-ray and radiation to diagnosing and treating disease. Radiologists direct an array of imaging technologies (such as ultrasound, computed tomography (CT), nuclear medicine, positron emission tomography (PET) and magnetic resonance imaging (MRI)) to diagnose or treat disease. Interventional Radiology is the performance of (usually minimally invasive) medical procedures with the guidance of imaging technologies.

CRAM101

Chapter 3. PART III: Chapter 9 - Chapter 13

Surgery	Surgery is a medical specialty that uses operative manual and instrumental techniques on a patient to investigate and/or treat a pathological condition such as disease or injury, to help improve bodily function or appearance, and sometimes for religious reasons. An act of performing Surgery may be called a surgical procedure, operation, or simply Surgery. In this context, the verb operating means performing Surgery.
Ethmoid bone	The Ethmoid bone is a bone in the skull that separates the nasal cavity from the brain. As such, it is located at the roof of the nose, between the two orbits. The cubical bone is lightweight due to a spongy construction.
Review of systems	A Review of systems is a component of an admission note covering the organ systems, with a focus upon the subjective symptoms perceived by the patient (as opposed to the objective signs perceived by the clinician). It can be particularly useful in identifying conditions that don`t have precise diagnostic tests. Whatever system a specific condition may seem restricted to, it may be reasonable to review all the other systems in a comprehensive history.
Family	Family is a group of people or animals (many species form the equivalent of a human Family wherein the adults care for the young) affiliated by consanguinity, affinity or co-residence. Although the concept of consanguinity originally referred to relations by `blood`, anthropologists have argued that one must understand the idea of `blood` metaphorically and that many societies understand Family through other concepts rather than through genetic distance. One of the primary functions of the Family is to produce and reproduce persons, biologically and socially.
Sphenoid bone	The Sphenoid bone is an unpaired bone situated at the base of the skull in front of the temporal bone and basilar part of the occipital bone. The Sphenoid bone is one of the seven bones that articulate to form the orbit. Its shape somewhat resembles that of a butterfly or bat with its wings extended. It is divided into the following parts:

· a median portion, known as the body of Sphenoid bone, containing the sella turcica which houses the pituitary gland

· two greater wings and two lesser wings

· Pterygoid processes of the sphenoides which project from it posteriorly
Two sphenoidal conchae are situated at the anterior and posterior part of the body.

Various other named features of the Sphenoid bone exist:

· pterygoid notch

· pterygoid fossa

· scaphoid fossa

· pterygoid hamulus

· pterygoid canal

· pterygospinous process
The Sphenoid bone of humans is homologous with a number of bones that are often separate in other animals, and have a somewhat complex arrangement.

Submandibular gland	The paired Submandibular glands are salivary glands located beneath the floor of the mouth. In humans, they account for 70% of the salivary volume and weigh about 15 grams.

Lying superior to the digastric muscles, each Submandibular gland is divided into superficial and deep lobes, which are separated by the mylohyoid muscle:

· The superficial portion is larger. The mylohyoid muscle runs below it.

	· The deep portion is smaller.
Emergency department	The Emergency department, also termed Accident ' Emergency (A'E), Emergency Room (ER), Emergency Ward (EW), or Casualty Department is a hospital or primary care department that provides initial treatment to patients with a broad spectrum of illnesses and injuries, some of which may be life-threatening and require immediate attention. In some countries, Emergency departments have become important entry points for those without other means of access to medical care. Staff teams treat emergency patients and provide support to family members.
Home care	Home care, (commonly referred to as domiciliary care), is health care , it is also known as skilled care) or by family and friends (also known as caregivers, primary caregiver, or voluntary caregivers who give informal care). Often, the term Home care is used to distinguish non-medical care or custodial care, which is care that is provided by persons who are not nurses, doctors, or other licensed medical personnel, whereas the term home health care, refers to care that is provided by licensed personnel. `Home care`, `home health care`, `in-Home care` are phrases that are used interchangeably in the United States to mean any type of care given to a person in their own home.
Case management	Case management refers to the coordination of services such as health, legal, or financial on behalf of a party. This typically includes creating a case file and following a process to ensure delivery of services. A case is handled by a case manager or case team.
Preventive medicine	Preventive medicine or preventive care refers to measures taken to prevent diseases, (or injuries) rather than curing them. It can be contrasted not only with curative medicine, but also with public health methods (which work at the level of population health rather than individual health). This takes place at primary, secondary and tertiary prevention levels.
Overnight	Overnight is a 2003 documentary by Tony Montana and Mark Brian Smith. The film details the rise and fall of filmmaker and musician Troy Duffy. Tagline: There`s more than one way to shoot yourself.
Risk factor	A Risk factor is a variable associated with an increased risk of disease or infection. Risk factors are correlational and not necessarily causal, because correlation does not imply causation. For example, being young cannot be said to cause measles, but young people are more at risk as they are less likely to have developed immunity during a previous epidemic.
Pediatrics	

· Children`s hospital

· Medical specialty

· Pediatric ophthalmology

· Pediatric endocrinology

· Child life specialist

· Contemporary Pediatrics - a monthly magazine

· Clinical Pediatrics - a peer-reviewed journal

· Pediatric Image Quiz - a collection of interesting images in Pediatrics

· American Academy of Pediatrics

· Baby Constipation? .

Anesthesia	Anesthesia has traditionally meant the condition of having sensation blocked or temporarily taken away. This allows patients to undergo surgery and other procedures without the distress and pain they would otherwise experience. The word was coined by Oliver Wendell Holmes, Sr.
Integumentary system	`Integument` redirects here; in botany, an integument is an outer membrane of an ovule, which later develops into a seed coat.
	The Integumentary system is the organ system that protects the body from damage, comprising the skin and its appendages . The Integumentary system has a variety of functions; it may serve to waterproof, cushion and protect the deeper tissues, excrete wastes, regulate temperature and is the attachment site for sensory receptors to detect pain, sensation, pressure and temperature.

Chapter 3. PART III: Chapter 9 - Chapter 13

Incision and drainage	Incision and drainage and clinical lancing are minor surgical procedures to release pus or pressure built up under the skin, such as from an abscess, boil, or infected paranasal sinus. It is performed by treating the area with an antiseptic, such as iodine based solution, and then making a small incision to puncture the skin using a sterile instrument such as a sharp needle, a pointed scalpel or a lancet. This allows the pus fluid to escape by draining out through the incision.
Biopsy	A Biopsy is a medical test involving the removal of cells or tissues for examination. It is the removal of tissue from a living subject to determine the presence or extent of a disease. The tissue is generally examined under a microscope by a pathologist, and can also be analyzed chemically.
Lesion	A Lesion is any abnormal tissue found on or in an organism, usually damaged by disease or trauma. Lesion is derived from the Latin word laesio which means injury. Lesions are caused by any process that damages tissues.
Nail	A nail is a horn-like structure at the end of a person's (or an animal's) finger or toe. The nail is generally regarded as a distinctively primate feature. Although it is not a feature confined exclusively to primates, the development of nails is extremely rare in other mammals.
Replacement	Replacement means: · Replacements, Tuttle, Lisa · Axiom schema of Replacement · Text Replacement, a feature of word processors correcting automatically common misspellings and typos · Replacement rate · Sampling (statistics) with Replacement .

Allograft	Allotransplantation is the transplantation of cells, tissues, or organs, sourced from a genetically non-identical member of the same species as the recipient.. The transplant is called an Allograft or allogeneic transplant or homograft. Most human tissue and organ transplants are Allografts.
Burn	A burn is a type of skin injury that may be caused by heat, electricity, chemicals, light, radiation, or friction. Most burns only affect the skin (epidermal tissue and dermis). Rarely deeper tissues, such as muscle, bone, and blood vessel can also be injured.
Pressure	Example reading: $1\ Pa = 1\ N/m^2 = 10^{-5}\ bar = 10.197\times10^{-6}\ at = 9.8692\times10^{-6}\ atm$, etc. As an example of varying Pressures, a finger can be pressed against a wall without making any lasting impression; however, the same finger pushing a thumbtack can easily damage the wall. Although the force applied to the surface is the same, the thumbtack applies more Pressure because the point concentrates that force into a smaller area.
Bedsores	Bedsores, more properly known as pressure ulcers or decubitus ulcers, are lesions caused by many factors such as: unrelieved pressure; friction; humidity; shearing forces; temperature; age; continence and medication; to any part of the body, especially portions over bony or cartilaginous areas such as sacrum, elbows, knees, ankles etc. Although easily prevented and completely treatable if found early, Bedsores are often fatal - even under the auspices of medical care - and are one of the leading iatrogenic causes of death reported in developed countries, second only to adverse drug reactions. Prior to the 1950s, treatment was ineffective until Doreen Norton showed that the primary cure and treatment was to remove the pressure by turning the patient every two hours.
Procedures	An ASC is a health care facility that specializes in providing surgery, including certain pain management and diagnostic (e.g., colonoscopy) services in an outpatient setting. Overall, the services provided can be generally called procedures. In simple terms, ASC-qualified procedures can be considered procedures that are more intensive than those done in the average doctor's office but not so intensive as to require a hospital stay.
Musculoskeletal system	A Musculoskeletal system is an organ system that gives animals (including humans) the ability to move using the muscular and skeletal systems. The Musculoskeletal system provides form, stability, and movement to the body.

	It is made up of the body's bones (the skeleton), muscles, cartilage, tendons, ligaments, joints, and other connective tissue (the tissue that supports and binds tissues and organs together).
Excision	Excision means 'removal by cutting'.
	· In surgery, an Excision is the complete removal of an organ, tissue, or tumor from a body, as opposed to a biopsy. An 'Excisional biopsy' (sometimes called a 'tumorectomy') is the removal of a tumor with a minimum of healthy tissue. It is therefore an Excision rather than a biopsy.
	· It is a term used by the Australian government as part of its definition of the Australian migration zone.
	· The Excision theorem is an important theorem in Algebraic topology, a branch of Mathematics.
Replantation	Replantation is the surgical reattachment of a body part, most commonly a finger, hand or arm, that has been completely cut from a person's body. Replantation of amputated parts has been performed in amputated fingers, hands, forearms, feet, amputated ears, avulsed scalp injuries, an amputated face, amputated lips, amputated penis and an amputated tongue.
	· eMedicine: Replantation
Arthrodesis	Arthrodesis is the artificial induction of joint ossification between two bones via surgery. This is done to relieve intractable pain in a joint which cannot be managed by pain medication, splints, or other normally-indicated treatments. The typical causes of such pain are fractures which disrupt the joint, and arthritis.
Respiratory system	The respiratory system's function is to allow gas exchange to all parts of the body. The space between the alveoli and the capillaries, the anatomy or structure of the exchange system, and the precise physiological uses of the exchanged gases vary depending on the organism. In humans and other mammals, for example, the anatomical features of the respiratory system include airways, lungs, and the respiratory muscles.
Larynx	The Larynx , colloquially known as the 'voice box', is an organ in the neck of mammals involved in protection of the trachea and sound production. It manipulates pitch and volume. The Larynx houses the vocal folds, which are an essential component of phonation.

Lung	The Lung or pulmonary system is the essential respiration organ in air-breathing animals, including most tetrapods, a few fish and a few snails. In mammals and the more complex life forms, the two Lungs are located in the chest on either side of the heart. Their principal function is to transport oxygen from the atmosphere into the bloodstream, and to release carbon dioxide from the bloodstream into the atmosphere.
Pleura	In human anatomy, the Pleural cavity is the body cavity that surrounds the lungs. The Pleura is a serous membrane which folds back upon itself to form a two-layered, membrane structure. The thin space between the two Pleural layers is known as the Pleural cavity; it normally contains a small amount of Pleural fluid.
Cardiovascular system	The circulatory system is an organ system that passes nutrients (such as amino acids and electrolytes), gases, hormones, blood cells, etc. to and from cells in the body to help fight diseases and help stabilize body temperature and pH to maintain homeostasis. This system may be seen strictly as a blood distribution network, but some consider the circulatory system as composed of the Cardiovascular system, which distributes blood, and the lymphatic system, which distributes lymph.
Vein	In the circulatory system, Veins are blood vessels that carry blood towards the heart. Most Veins carry deoxygenated blood from the tissues back to the lungs; exceptions are the pulmonary and umbilical Veins, both of which carry oxygenated blood. They differ from arteries in structure and function; for example, arteries are more muscular than Veins and they carry blood away from the heart.
Arteriovenous fistula	An Arteriovenous fistula is an abnormal connection or passageway between an artery and a vein. It may be congenital, surgically created for hemodialysis treatments, or acquired due to pathologic process, such as trauma or erosion of an arterial aneurysm. A radiocephalic fistula. Patients with end stage renal failure are treated with hemodialysis.
Fistula	In medicine, a Fistula (pl. Fistulas or Fistulae) is an abnormal connection or passageway between two epithelium-lined organs or vessels that normally do not connect. It is generally a disease condition, but a Fistula may be surgically created for therapeutic reasons.
Brachytherapy	Brachytherapy , also known as sealed source radiotherapy or endocurietherapy, is a form of radiotherapy where a radioactive source is placed inside or next to the area requiring treatment. Brachytherapy is commonly used to treat localized prostate cancer, cervical cancer and cancers of the head and neck. Brachytherapy to prevent restenosis after stenting associated with coronary angioplasty has been proven safe and effective in clinicals trials, such as the START and START 40/20 Trials.

Monitoring	To monitor or Monitoring generally means to be aware of the state of a system. Below are specific examples: · to observe a situation for any changes which may occur over time, using a monitor or measuring device of some sort: · Baby monitor, medical monitor, Heart rate monitor · BioMonitoring · Cure Monitoring for composite materials manufacturing · Deformation Monitoring · Election Monitoring · Mining Monitoring · Natural hazard Monitoring · Network Monitoring · Structural Monitoring · Website Monitoring · Futures Monitoring, Media Monitoring service · to observe the behaviour or communications of individuals or groups · Monitoring competence at a task. · Clinical Monitoring for new medical drugs Monitoring Integration Platform

· Indiktor - Monitoring Integration Platform

.

Cardiac catheterization	Cardiac catheterization (heart cath) is the insertion of a catheter into a chamber or vessel of the heart. This is done for both investigational and interventional purposes. Coronary catheterization is a subset of this technique, involving the catheterization of the coronary arteries.
Blood pressure	Blood pressure is the pressure (force per unit area) exerted by circulating blood on the walls of blood vessels, and constitutes one of the principal vital signs. The pressure of the circulating blood decreases as it moves away from the heart through arteries and capillaries, and toward the heart through veins. When unqualified, the term Blood pressure usually refers to brachial arterial pressure: that is, in the major blood vessel of the upper left or right arm that takes blood away from the heart.
Urinary system	The Urinary system is the organ system that produces, stores, and eliminates urine. In humans it includes two kidneys, two ureters, the bladder, the urethra, and the penis in males. The analogous organ in invertebrates is the nephridium.
Intersex	Intersex in humans refers to intermediate or atypical combinations of physical features that usually distinguish female from male. This is usually understood to be congenital, involving chromosomal, morphologic, genital and/or gonadal anomalies, such as diversion from typical XX-female or XY-male presentations, e.g., sex reversal (XY-female, XX-male), genital ambiguity, sex developmental differences. An Intersex individual may have biological characteristics of both the male and female sexes.
Intersex surgery	Intersex surgery is one of several terms referring to surgery performed to correct birth defects or early injuries of the genitalia, primarily for the purposes of making the appearance more normal and to reduce the likelihood of future problems. The recent history of Intersex surgery has been characterized by controversy after publicized reports that surgery failed to achieve the desired outcomes in many cases. Timing of surgery (infancy, adolescence or adult age) has also been controversial.
Auditory	Auditory means of or relating to the process of hearing:

· Auditory system, the neurological structures and pathways of sound perception.

· Sound, the physical signal perceived by the Auditory system.

· Hearing (sense), is the Auditory sense, the sense by which sound is perceived.

· Ear, the Auditory end organ.

· Cochlea, the Auditory branch of the inner ear.

· Auditory illusion, sound trick analogous to an optical illusion.

· Primary Auditory cortex, the part of the higher-level of the brain that serves hearing.

· External Auditory meatus, the ear canal

· Auditory scene analysis, the process by which a scene containing many sounds is perceived

· Auditory phonetics, the science of the sounds of language

· Auditory imagery, hearing in head in the absence of sound

Auditory system	The Auditory system is the sensory system for the sense of hearing.
	The folds of cartilage surrounding the ear canal are called the pinna. Sound waves are reflected and attenuated when they hit the pinna, and these changes provide additional information that will help the brain determine the direction from which the sounds came.
Ultrasound	Ultrasound is cyclic sound pressure with a frequency greater than the upper limit of human hearing. Although this limit varies from person to person, it is approximately 20 kilohertz (20,000 hertz) in healthy, young adults and thus, 20 kHz serves as a useful lower limit in describing Ultrasound. The production of Ultrasound is used in many different fields, typically to penetrate a medium and measure the reflection signature or supply focused energy.

Radiation	In physics, Radiation describes any process in which energy travels through a medium or through space, ultimately to be absorbed by another body. Non-physicists often associate the word ionizing Radiation but it can also refer to electromagnetic Radiation which can also be ionizing Radiation, to acoustic Radiation, or to other more obscure processes. What makes it Radiation is that the energy radiates (i.e., it travels outward in straight lines in all directions) from the source.
Mammography	Mammography is the process of using low-dose amplitude-X-rays (usually around 0.7 mSv) to examine the human breast and is used as a diagnostic as well as a screening tool. The goal of Mammography is the early detection of breast cancer, typically through detection of characteristic masses and/or microcalcifications. Mammography is believed to reduce mortality from breast cancer.
Oncology	Oncology is the branch of medicine dealing with tumors (cancer). A medical professional who practices Oncology is an oncologist. The term originates from the Greek `Ογκολογΐα` derived from onkos , meaning bulk, mass, or tumor, and the suffix -logy (-λογΐα), meaning `study of` or `to talk about`.
Nuclear medicine	Nuclear medicine is a branch or specialty of medicine and medical imaging that uses radioactive isotopes (radionuclides) and relies on the process of radioactive decay in the diagnosis and treatment of disease. In Nuclear medicine procedures, radionuclides are combined with other chemical compounds or pharmaceuticals to form (radiopharmaceuticals). These radiopharmaceuticals, once administered to the patient, can localize to specific organs or cellular receptors.
Cytogenetic	Cytogenetics is a branch of genetics that is concerned with the study of the structure and function of the cell, especially the chromosomes. It includes routine analysis of G-Banded chromosomes, other Cytogenetic banding techniques, as well as molecular Cytogenetics such as fluorescent in situ hybridization (FISH) and comparative genomic hybridization (CGH). Chromosomes were first observed in plant cells by Karl Wilhelm von Nägeli in 1842. Their behavior in animal (salamander) cells was described by Walther Flemming, the discoverer of mitosis, in 1882. The name was coined by another German anatomist, von Waldeyer in 1888.
Thalamus	The Thalamus is a midline paired symmetrical structure within the brains of vertebrates, including humans. It is situated between the cerebral cortex and midbrain, both in terms of location and neurological connections. Its function includes relaying sensation, special sense and motor signals to the cerebral cortex, along with the regulation of consciousness, sleep and alertness.

CLAM101

Chapter 3. PART III: Chapter 9 - Chapter 13

Hematology	Hematology, also spelled haematology, is the branch of internal medicine, physiology, pathology, clinical laboratory work, and pediatrics that is concerned with the study of blood, the blood-forming organs, and blood diseases. Hematology includes the study of etiology, diagnosis, treatment, prognosis, and prevention of blood diseases. The laboratology work that goes into the study of blood is frequently performed by a medical technologist.
Urinalysis	A Urinalysis is an array of tests performed on urine and one of the most common methods of medical diagnosis. A part of a Urinalysis can be performed by using urine dipsticks, in which the test results can be read as color changes. A typical medical Urinalysis usually includes: · a description of color and appearance.
Coagulation	Coagulation is a complex process by which blood forms clots. It is an important part of hemostasis , wherein a damaged blood vessel wall is covered by a platelet and fibrin-containing clot to stop bleeding and begin repair of the damaged vessel. Disorders of Coagulation can lead to an increased risk of bleeding (hemorrhage) or clotting (thrombosis).
Immunology	Immunology is a broad branch of biomedical science that covers the study of all aspects of the immune system in all organisms. It deals with, among other things, the physiological functioning of the immune system in states of both health and disease; malfunctions of the immune system in immunological disorders (autoimmune diseases, hypersensitivities, immune deficiency, transplant rejection); the physical, chemical and physiological characteristics of the components of the immune system in vitro, in situ, and in vivo. Immunology has applications in several disciplines of science, and as such is further divided.
Microbiology	Microbiology is the study of microorganisms, which are unicellular or cell-cluster microscopic organisms. This includes eukaryotes such as fungi and protists, and prokaryotes. Viruses, though not strictly classed as living organisms, are also studied.
Tissue typing	Tissue typing is a procedure in which the tissues of a prospective donor and recipient are tested for compatibility prior to transplantation. An embryo can be tissue typed to ensure that the embryo implanted can be a cord-blood stem cell donor for a sick sibling. One technique of Tissue typing, `mixed leukocyte reaction`, is performed by culturing lymphocytes from the donor together with those from the recipient.

Transfusion	Blood Transfusion is the process of transferring blood or blood-based products from one person into the circulatory system of another. Blood Transfusions can be life-saving in some situations, such as massive blood loss due to trauma, or can be used to replace blood lost during surgery. Blood Transfusions may also be used to treat a severe anaemia or thrombocytopenia caused by a blood disease.
Cytopathology	Cytopathology is a branch of pathology that studies and diagnoses diseases on the cellular level. The discipline was founded by Rudolf Virchow in 1858. A common application of Cytopathology is the Pap smear, used as a screening tool, to detect precancerous cervical lesions and prevent cervical cancer.
Surgical	Surgery is a medical specialty that uses operative manual and instrumental techniques on a patient to investigate and/or treat a pathological condition such as disease or injury, to help improve bodily function or appearance, or sometimes for some other reason. An act of performing surgery may be called a surgical procedure, operation, or simply surgery. In this context, the verb operating means performing surgery.
Surgical pathology	Surgical pathology is the most significant and time-consuming area of practice for most anatomical pathologists. Surgical pathology involves the gross and microscopic examination of surgical specimens, as well as biopsies submitted by non-surgeons such as general internists, medical subspecialists, dermatologists, and interventional radiologists. The practice of Surgical pathology allows for definitive diagnosis of disease (or lack thereof) in any case where tissue is surgically removed from a patient.
Immunization	Immunization is the process by which an individual`s immune system becomes fortified against an agent (known as the immunogen). When an immune system is exposed to molecules that are foreign to the body (non-self), it will orchestrate an immune response, but it can also develop the ability to quickly respond to a subsequent encounter (through immunological memory). This is a function of the adaptive immune system.
Vaccine	A Vaccine is a biological preparation that improves immunity to a particular disease. A Vaccine typically contains a small amount of an agent that resembles a microorganism. The agent stimulates the body`s immune system to recognize the agent as foreign, destroy it, and `remember` it, so that the immune system can more easily recognize and destroy any of these microorganisms that it later encounters.

Biofeedback	Biofeedback is a non-medical process that involves measuring a subject's specific and quantifiable bodily functions such as blood pressure, heart rate, skin temperature, sweat gland activity, and muscle tension, conveying the information to the patient in real-time. This raises the patient's awareness and therefore the possibility of conscious control of those functions. By providing the user access to physiological information about which he or she may be unaware, Biofeedback may allow users to gain control of physical processes previously considered an automatic response of the autonomous nervous system.
Dialysis	In medicine, Dialysis is primarily used to provide an artificial replacement for lost kidney function due to renal failure. Dialysis may be used for very sick patients who have suddenly but temporarily, lost their kidney function (acute renal failure) or for quite stable patients who have permanently lost their kidney function (stage 5 chronic kidney disease). When healthy, the kidneys maintain the body's internal equilibrium of water and minerals (sodium, potassium, chloride, calcium, phosphorus, magnesium, sulfate) and the kidneys remove from the blood the daily metabolic load of fixed hydrogen ions.
Hemodialysis	In medicine, Hemodialysis is a method for removing waste products such as creatinine and urea, as well as free water from the blood when the kidneys are in renal failure. Hemodialysis is one of three renal replacement therapies (the other two being renal transplant; peritoneal dialysis). Hemodialysis can be an outpatient or inpatient therapy.
Psychiatry	Psychiatry is a medical specialty officially devoted to the treatment and study of mental disorders. The term was first coined by the German physician Johann Christian Reil in 1808. Psychiatric assessment typically involves a mental status examination, the taking of a case history.
Gastroenterology	Gastroenterology (MeSH heading) is the branch of medicine whereby the digestive system and its disorders are studied. Etymologically, the name is a combination of three Ancient Greek words gastros , enteron (intestine), and logos (reason). Diseases affecting the gastrointestinal tract, which includes the organs from mouth to anus, along the alimentary canal, are the focus of this specialty.
Ophthalmology	Ophthalmology is the branch of medicine which deals with the diseases and surgery of the visual pathways, including the eye, hairs, and areas surrounding the eye, such as the lacrimal system and eyelids. The term ophthalmologist is an eye specialist for medical and surgical problems. Since ophthalmologists perform operations on eyes, they are considered to be both a surgical and medical specialty.

Allergy	Allergy is a disorder of the immune system often also referred to as atopy. Allergic reactions occur to normally harmless environmental substances known as allergens; these reactions are acquired, predictable, and rapid. Strictly, Allergy is one of four forms of hypersensitivity and is called type I (or immediate) hypersensitivity.
Clinical	Clinical can refer to: · clinical medical practice · Clinic · Illness · clinical waste, segregated for safety or security · clinical medical professions · clinical psychology · clinical examination; see Physical examination

· clinical conditions, diagnosed from clinical examination alone

· clinical death

· clinical research

· clinical governance of patient care within a health system

· clinical trial, research involving patients

· clinical linguistics, linguistics applied to speech therapy .

Genetics	Genetics a discipline of biology, is the science of heredity and variation in living organisms. The fact that living things inherit traits from their parents has been used since prehistoric times to improve crop plants and animals through selective breeding. However, the modern science of Genetics, which seeks to understand the process of inheritance, only began with the work of Gregor Mendel in the mid-nineteenth century.
Chemotherapy	Chemotherapy, in its most general sense, refers to treatment of disease by chemicals that kill cells, both good and bad, but specifically those of micro-organisms or cancerous tumours. In popular usage, it refers to antineoplastic drugs used to treat cancer or the combination of these drugs into a cytotoxic standardized treatment regimen. In its non-oncological use, the term may also refer to antibiotics (antibacterial Chemotherapy).
Infusion	An Infusion is the outcome of steeping plants with a desired flavour in water or oil.

373

The first recorded use of essential oils was in the 10th or 11th century by the Persian polymath Avicenna, possibly in the Canon of Medicine.

An Infusion is very similar to a decoction but is used with herbs that are more volatile or dissolve readily in water, or release their active ingredients easily in oil.

Photodynamic therapy	Photodynamic therapy (PDT), matured as a feasible medical technology in the 1980s at several institutions throughout the world, is a third-level treatment for cancer involving three key components: a photosensitizer, light, and tissue oxygen. It is also being investigated for treatment of psoriasis, and is an approved treatment for wet macular degeneration. The German physician Friedrich Meyer-Betz performed the first study with what was first called photoradiation therapy with porphyrins in humans in 1913.
Heart	The Heart is a muscular organ found in most vertebrates that is responsible for pumping blood throughout the blood vessels by repeated, rhythmic contractions. The term cardiac (as in cardiology) means `related to the Heart` and comes from the Greek καρδιῆ, kardia, for `Heart.` The vertebrate Heart is composed of cardiac muscle, an involuntary striated muscle tissue which is found only within this organ. The average human Heart, beating at 72 beats per minute, will beat approximately 2.5 billion times during a lifetime (about 66 years).
Heart failure	Heart failure is a condition in which a problem with the structure or function of the heart impairs its ability to supply sufficient blood flow to meet the body`s needs. It should not be confused with cardiac arrest . Common causes of Heart failure include myocardial infarction and other forms of ischemic heart disease, hypertension, valvular heart disease and cardiomyopathy.
Sedation	Sedation is a medical procedure involving the administration of sedative drugs, generally to facilitate a medical procedure with local anaesthesia. Sedation is now typically used in procedures such as endoscopy, vasectomy,RSI (Rapid Sequence Intubation), or minor surgery and in dentistry for reconstructive surgery, some cosmetic surgeries, removal of wisdom teeth, or for high-anxiety patients. Sedation methods in dentistry include inhalation Sedation (using nitrous oxide), oral Sedation, and intravenous (IV) Sedation.
Hepatitis A	Hepatitis A is an acute infectious disease of the liver caused by the Hepatitis A virus (HAV), which is most commonly transmitted by the fecal-oral route via contaminated food or drinking water. Every year, approximately 10 million people worldwide are infected with the virus. The time between infection and the appearance of the symptoms, (the incubation period), is between two and six weeks and the average incubation period is 28 days.

Clam101

Hepatitis B	Hepatitis B is a disease caused by Hepatitis B virus (HBV) which infects the liver of hominoidae, including humans, and causes an inflammation called hepatitis. Originally known as `serum hepatitis`, the disease has caused epidemics in parts of Asia and Africa, and it is endemic in China. About a third of the world`s population, more than 2 billion people, have been infected with the Hepatitis B virus.
Local	Local usually refers to something nearby, or in the immediate area.
	It may be used in many ways, some of which are related to this general meaning, others which are not:
	.
Nasal cavity	The Nasal cavity is a large fluid filled space above and behind the nose in the middle of the face.
	The Nasal cavity conditions the air to be received by the other areas of the respiratory tract. Owing to the large surface area provided by the conchae, the air passing through the Nasal cavity is warmed or cooled to within 1 degree of body temperature.
Nasopharynx	The Nasopharynx is the uppermost part of the pharynx. It extends from the base of the skull to the upper surface of the soft palate; it differs from the oral and laryngeal parts of the pharynx in that its cavity always remains patent (open).
	In front it communicates through the choanae with the nasal cavities.
Disease	A Disease or medical condition is an abnormal condition of an organism that impairs bodily functions, associated with specific symptoms and signs. It may be caused by external factors, such as invading organisms, or it may be caused by internal dysfunctions, such as autoimmune Diseases. In human beings, `Disease` is often used more broadly to refer to any condition that causes pain, dysfunction, distress, social problems, and/or death to the person afflicted, or similar problems for those in contact with the person.
Guideline	`Guideline` is the NATO reporting name for the Soviet SA-2 surface-to-air missile.

	A Guideline is any document that aims to streamline particular processes according to a set routine. By definition, following a Guideline is never mandatory (protocol would be a better term for a mandatory procedure).
Late effect	In medicine, a Late effect is a condition that appears after the acute phase of an earlier, causal condition has run its course. A Late effect can be caused directly by the earlier condition, or indirectly by the treatment for the earlier condition. Some Late effects can occur decades later.
Neoplasm	Neoplasm is an abnormal mass of tissue as a result of neoplasia. Neoplasia is the abnormal proliferation of cells. The growth of this clone of cells exceeds, and is uncoordinated with, that of the normal tissues around it.
Endocrine diseases	Among the hundreds of Endocrine diseases (or endocrinological diseases) are: · Adrenal disorders: · Adrenal insufficiency · Addison`s disease  · Congenital adrenal hyperplasia (adrenogenital syndrome)  · Mineralocorticoid deficiency  · Conn`s syndrome · Cushing`s syndrome · adrenogenital syndrome · Pheochromocytoma · Adrenocortical carcinoma

Cram101

· GRA/Glucocorticoid remediable aldosteronism

· Glucose homeostasis disorders:

· Diabetes mellitus

· Hypoglycemia

· Idiopathic hypoglycemia

· Insulinoma

· Metabolic bone disease:

· Osteoporosis

· Osteitis deformans (Paget`s disease of bone)

· Rickets and osteomalacia

· Pituitary gland disorders:

· Diabetes insipidus

· Hypopituitarism (or Panhypopituitarism)

· Pituitary tumors

· Pituitary adenomas

· Prolactinoma (or Hyperprolactinemia)

· Acromegaly, gigantism

· Cushing`s disease

· Parathyroid gland disorders:

· Primary hyperparathyroidism

· Secondary hyperparathyroidism

· Tertiary hyperparathyroidism

· Hypoparathyroidism

· Pseudohypoparathyroidism

· Sex hormone disorders:

· Disorders of sex development or intersex disorders

· Hermaphroditism

· Gonadal dysgenesis

· Androgen insensitivity syndromes

· Hypogonadism

· Gonadotropin deficiency

· Kallmann syndrome

· Klinefelter syndrome

· Ovarian failure

· Testicular failure

· Turner syndrome

· Disorders of Gender

· Gender identity disorder

· Disorders of Puberty

· Delayed puberty

· Precocious puberty

· Menstrual function or fertility disorders

· Amenorrhea

· Polycystic ovary syndrome

· Thyroid disorders:

· Goiter

· Hyperthyroidism and Graves-Basedow disease

· Hypothyroidism

· Thyroiditis

· Thyroid cancer

· Tumours of the endocrine glands not mentioned elsewhere

· Multiple endocrine neoplasia

· MEN type 1

· MEN type 2a

· MEN type 2b

· .

Childbirth	Childbirth (, birth, partus or parturition) is the culmination of a human pregnancy or gestation period with birth of one or more newborn infants from a woman`s uterus. The process of normal human Childbirth is categorized in three stages of labour: the shortening and dilation of the cervix, descent and birth of the infant, and birth of the placenta.. In some cases, Childbirth is achieved through caesarean section, the removal of the neonate through a surgical incision in the abdomen, rather than through vaginal birth.
Genitourinary system	In anatomy, the Genitourinary system or urogenital system is the organ system of the reproductive organs and the urinary system. These are grouped together because of their proximity to each other, their common embryological origin and the use of common pathways, like the male urethra. Also, because of their proximity, the systems are sometimes imaged together.
Pregnancy	Pregnancy is the carrying of one or more offspring, known as a fetus or embryo, inside the uterus of a female. In a pregnancy, there can be multiple gestations, as in the case of twins or triplets. Human pregnancy is the most studied of all mammalian pregnancies.
Puerperium	Postnatal is the period beginning immediately after the birth of a child and extending for about six weeks. Another term would be postpartum period, as it refers to the mother . Less frequently used is Puerperium.
Symptoms	A symptom is a departure from normal function or feeling which is noticed by a patient, indicating the presence of disease or abnormality. A symptom is subjective, observed by the patient, and not measured. Symptoms may be chronic, relapsing or remitting.

Regurgitation	Regurgitation, Regurgiate or Regurgitate can refer to:
	· Regurgitation
	· Vomiting
	· Regurgitation
	· Regurgitate (band), a goregrind band `
Epiglottis	The Epiglottis is a flap of elastic cartilage tissue covered with a mucus membrane, attached to the root of the tongue. It projects obliquely upwards behind the tongue and the hyoid bone. The term is, like tonsils, often incorrectly used to refer to the uvula.
Superficial	Superficial is an adjective generally meaning `regarding the surface`, often metaphorically. Both in the literal as in the metaphorical sense the term has often a negative connotation based on the idea that deeper parts are also important to consider.
	· In human anatomy, Superficial describes objects near the body`s surface as compared to other objects that may be deep. For example, skin is a Superficial structure of the body and muscles are deep to skin.

Renal vein	Latin	venae renales
Gray`s	subject #173 679	
Drains from	kidney	
Source	interlobar veins	
Drains to	inferior vena cava	
Artery	Renal artery	
MeSH	Renal+Veins	

Go to **Cram101.com** for Interactive Practice Exams for this book or virtually any of your books.
And, **NEVER** highlight a book again!

The Renal veins are veins that drain the kidney. They connect the kidney to the inferior vena cava.

It is usually singular to each kidney, except in the condition `multiple Renal veins`.

It also divides into 2 divisions upon entering the kidney:

· the anterior branch which receives blood from the anterior portion of the kidney and,

· the posterior branch which receives blood from the posterior portion.

| Pelvis | In human anatomy, the pelvis is the part of the trunk inferioposterior to the abdomen in the transition area between the trunk and the lower limbs. The term is used to denote several structures: |

In human anatomy, the pelvis is the part of the trunk inferioposterior to the abdomen in the transition area between the trunk and the lower limbs. The term is used to denote several structures:

· the pelvic girdle or bony pelvis, the irregular ring-shaped bony structure connecting the spine to the femurs,

· the pelvic cavity, the space enclosed by the pelvic girdle, subdivided into

· the greater or false pelvis and

· the lesser or true pelvis which provides the skeletal framework for the perineum and the pelvic cavity (which are separated by the pelvic diaphragm),

· the pelvic region.
`pelvis` is the Latin word for a `basin` and the pelvis thus got its name from its shape. It is also known as hip girdle or coxa girdle.

Tongue

The Tongue is a muscle on the floor of the mouth that manipulates food for chewing and swallowing (deglutition). It is the primary organ of taste, as much of the upper surface of the Tongue is covered in papillae and taste buds. A secondary function of the Tongue is speech, in which the organ assists.

CPSIA information can be obtained at www.ICGtesting.com
Printed in the USA
269258BV00003B/20/P